MW00523093

A HOME FULL OF MERCY

Visit our web site at
www.stpauls.us

or call 1-800-343-2522
and request current catalog

A HOME FULL OF
MERCY

THE GOSPEL OF LUKE IN THE FAMILY:
A STUDY GUIDE

VINCENZO PAGLIA

Translated by Edmund C. Lane, SSP

ST PAULS

First published in Italy in 2015 under the title
Una Casa Ricca di Misericordia: Il Vangelo di Luca in Famiglia
© EDIZIONE SAN PAOLO s.r.l. – Cinisello Balsamo (MI).

English language edition © 2015 by the Society of St. Paul

English translation by Edmund C. Lane, SSP

Library of Congress Cataloging-in-Publication Data

Paglia, Vincenzo.
  [Casa ricca di misericordia: English]
  A home full of mercy : the gospel of Luke in the family: a study guide /
Vincenzo Paglia.
    pages cm
    ISBN 978-0-8189-1389-1
  1. Bible. Luke—Meditations. 2. Families—Religious life. 3. Catholic
Church—Doctrines. I. Title.
    BS2595.54P3413 2015
    226.4'0071—dc23
                              2015027650

Produced and designed in the United States of America by the
Fathers and Brothers of the Society of St. Paul,
2187 Victory Boulevard, Staten Island, New York 10314-6603
as part of their communications apostolate.

ISBN 978-0-8189-1389-1

© Copyright 2015 by the Society of St. Paul

Current Printing - first digit   1   2   3   4   5   6   7   8   9   1 0

Place of Publication:
2187 Victory Blvd., Staten Island, NY 10314 - USA

Year of Current Printing - first year shown

2015   2016   2017   2018   2019   2020   2021   2022   2023   2024

Table of Contents

Biblical Abbreviations

OLD TESTAMENT

Genesis	Gn	Nehemiah	Ne	Baruch	Ba
Exodus	Ex	Tobit	Tb	Ezekiel	Ezk
Leviticus	Lv	Judith	Jdt	Daniel	Dn
Numbers	Nb	Esther	Est	Hosea	Ho
Deuteronomy	Dt	1 Maccabees	1 M	Joel	Jl
Joshua	Jos	2 Maccabees	2 M	Amos	Am
Judges	Jg	Job	Jb	Obadiah	Ob
Ruth	Rt	Psalms	Ps	Jonah	Jon
1 Samuel	1 S	Proverbs	Pr	Micah	Mi
2 Samuel	2 S	Ecclesiastes	Ec	Nahum	Na
1 Kings	1 K	Song of Songs	Sg	Habakkuk	Hab
2 Kings	2 K	Wisdom	Ws	Zephaniah	Zp
1 Chronicles	1 Ch	Sirach	Si	Haggai	Hg
2 Chronicles	2 Ch	Isaiah	Is	Malachi	Ml
Ezra	Ezr	Jeremiah	Jr	Zechariah	Zc
		Lamentations	Lm		

NEW TESTAMENT

Matthew	Mt	Ephesians	Eph	Hebrews	Heb
Mark	Mk	Philippians	Ph	James	Jm
Luke	Lk	Colossians	Col	1 Peter	1 P
John	Jn	1 Thessalonians	1 Th	2 Peter	2 P
Acts	Ac	2 Thessalonians	2 Th	1 John	1 Jn
Romans	Rm	1 Timothy	1 Tm	2 John	2 Jn
1 Corinthians	1 Cor	2 Timothy	2 Tm	3 John	3 Jn
2 Corinthians	2 Cor	Titus	Tt	Jude	Jude
Galatians	Gal	Philemon	Phm	Revelation	Rv

Introduction
The Gospel in the Home

Dear families,

I want to offer to each one of you this little book whose purpose is to help you in the reading of the Gospel of Luke at home in the family every day. This Gospel – called by many the "Gospel of Mercy" – was highlighted by Pope Francis as one which ought to accompany us in a special way during the Jubilee of Mercy in 2016.

Pope Francis in the Bull of Indiction officially proclaiming the Extraordinary Jubilee of Mercy writes:

> In the Gospel of Luke we find another important element that will help us live the Jubilee with faith. Luke writes that Jesus, on the Sabbath, went back to Nazareth and, as was his custom, entered the synagogue. They called upon him to read the Scripture and to comment on it. The passage was from the prophet Isaiah where it is written: "The Spirit of the Lord is upon me, because he has anointed me to bring glad tidings to the poor. He has sent me to proclaim liberty to captives and recovery of sight to the blind, to let the oppressed go free, and to proclaim a year acceptable to the Lord" (Lk 4:18-19).

At this point, Pope Francis continues:

A year of mercy: this is what the Lord proclaimed and that we want to live now. This Holy Year will bring to the fore the richness of the mission of Jesus which resounds in the words of the prophet: to bring a word and a gesture of consolation to the poor, to proclaim freedom to those who are bound by new forms of slavery in modern society, to restore sight to those who are no longer able to see because they are caught up in themselves, and to restore dignity to those who have been robbed of it. The preaching of Jesus is made visible once again in the response of faith which Christians are called to offer by their witness. May the words of the Apostle accompany us: "If one performs acts of mercy, let them be done cheerfully" (Rm 12:8).

We must start by listening to the Gospel

Every Christian generation – hence, also our own – is called to take this little book in hand. The Gospel is in fact the strength of the Church; it is the Word from which it was born and through which it lives. Christianity began, as a matter of fact, when the Word became flesh in the womb of Mary. She is the first believer and was at once pointed out as such by Elizabeth: "Blessed are you who believed that what was spoken to you by the Lord would be fulfilled" (Lk 1:45). And, after her, came the first disciples. When they embraced the word of Jesus a new fraternity began, we could say a "new family": that of Jesus with his disciples. After Pentecost the Gospel began to reach into the homes and families of Christians. Thus the course of the Gospel at the beginning of the first century was marked by its being listened to in families. Dear families, I believe that also at the beginning of this third millennium we need to revisit that which happened at the beginning of Christianity: once again take the Gospel in our hands, also in our families, and knit together a new fraternity among persons, a new solidarity between families, in order to be able to give the "good news" of the love of God to everyone. St. John Paul II, opening the great Jubilee of the Year 2000, pleaded with Christians to enter "into the new century with the book of the Gospels!" With that passion which made him a pilgrim for the Gospel all around the world he added: "Let us take this Book into our hands! Let us accept it from the Lord who continuously offers it to us by means of his Church (cf. Rv 10:8). Let us devour it so that it becomes the life of our life. Let us savor it in its depths: it will take some effort, but it will give us joy because it is as sweet as honey (cf. Rv 10:9-10). We will be filled to overflowing with hope and the ability to communicate it to every man and woman whom we meet on our journey."

Dear families, Pope Francis points us in this same direction: take the Gospel in hand! He says this in the wonderful letter entitled "The Joy of the Gospel" (*Evangelii gaudium*). It is indeed indispensable to pick up the Gospel and to listen to it with renewed attention in order to have a more fraternal, more united, more human world. The insecurity and fear which mark life in this world of ours, the incredible injustice that tears at the fabric of life of so many people, the violence that continues to reap innocent victims, can be overcome only thanks to the Gospel. Unfortunately, we believers risk being among those who do not believe in the power of the Gospel and who find ourselves changing and resigning ourselves to the sadness of the times. It is urgent to take up again and to listen with passion to the "good news," beginning in our families. There is a special grace when we read the Gospel in the family because it fulfills that which Jesus said: *"Where two or three are gathered together in my name, there am I in the midst of them* and whatever they ask for in prayer my Father will grant it to them" (Mt 18:20).

The Gospels, the Church's Treasure

Dear families, the exhortation to pick up the Gospel is not a frivolous invitation. The Gospel is the very heart of the biblical revelation, the most precious treasure of the Church. The Second Vatican Council, in *Dei Verbum*, writes: "Among all the Scriptures [...] the Gospels deservedly excel insofar as they constitute the principal testimony relative to the life and doctrine of the Word Incarnate, our Savior." For this reason, paraphrasing a saying of St. Jerome, we can say: "Ignorance of the Gospel is ignorance of Christ." The four Gospels are the richest and surest fount for knowing Jesus and for loving him. It is for this reason that they were written. The author of the Fourth Gospel, at the end of his work writes: *Jesus did many other signs in the presence of his disciples that are not written in this book. But these have been written so that you may come to believe that Jesus is the Messiah, the Son of God and that, through this belief, you may have life in his name* (Jn 20:30-31).

The evangelists were not interested in composing a detailed and actual biography of Jesus, but so that from these books the readers would be led in every time to the faith. In the Gospels, obviously, real facts that occurred are narrated, even if each one of the evangelists may have organized them according to his own particular plan. The conciliar document *Dei Verbum* sums up their origins in this way:

After the Ascension of the Lord the Apostles handed on to their hearers what He had said and done. This they did with that clearer understanding which they enjoyed after they had been instructed by the glorious events of Christ's life and been taught by the light of the Spirit of truth. The sacred authors wrote the four Gospels, selecting some things from among the many which had been handed on by word of mouth or in writing, reducing some of them to a synthesis, explaining some others in view of the particular situation of their own churches, while in the end preserving the form of proclamation but always in such a way as to speak about Jesus with sincerity and truth. Their intention in writing was that either from their own memory and recollections, or from the witness of those who "themselves from the beginning were eyewitnesses and ministers of the Word" we might know "the truth" concerning those matters about which we have been instructed (see Lk 1:2-4).

The Gospels enable us to meet Jesus

It is abundantly clear, therefore, why the four Gospels were written. They put us into contact with Jesus. They are not books like all the rest, because they make Jesus present as he speaks to those who listen. From this listening we receive a grace-filled energy, an interior power, mysterious but very real that changes, heals, transforms and saves us. The Gospel is the most precious treasure of the Church. Everyone should read it: believers and non-believers, children and the aged, young people and adults, the healthy and the sick, the just and the unjust, saints and sinners, free persons and prisoners, men and women, everyone. And it should especially be read in the family.

This little book has brought about an increase in faith throughout the world and has supported countless groups of believers for more than twenty centuries. It has been, in fact, two thousand years since this word was first announced to everyone. And, from then on, whoever listened to it was no longer the same person as before. The world itself is no longer the same since then. The Gospel has been the good yeast that has fermented the dough of the world and that continues to ferment it still. The Gospels are the light which illuminates mankind's steps toward peace. One does not listen to it once and for all because we always have need of yeast and light. In the Gospels is contained the living Word that accompanies the believer each day. Every generation is called to embrace and confront itself with this Word. Every family should prepare the table of the Gospel, that is, to listen to one page of it each day. Those who don't do this will not be able to know, much less, to love Jesus.

This little book contains the thought of Jesus, his heart, his compassion, his meekness, his strength. The heart of those who listen to him will become strong. What Peter experienced after an exhausting night on the lake without catching any fish happens to us too. Early in the morning the Lord appeared and told him to throw out his nets once more. Peter, even though he was exhausted, replied: "At your word I will throw out my nets" (Lk 5:5). And there was a miraculous catch of fish. Those who listen to the Gospel will always have a miraculous catch.

Even those who believe very little are invited to read the Gospel: they will come to know in depth the beauty of a love that loves without end, without setting any limits. And everyone will discover the truth of what Jesus said at the end of his sermon on the mountain, namely: "Everyone who listens to these words of mine and acts on them will be like a wise man who built his house on rock. The rain fell, the floods came, and the winds blew and buffeted the house. But it did not collapse; it had been set solidly on rock" (Mt 7:24-25). If we want to build the life of our family on a solid foundation, and the same holds true for the whole of society, we will start by nourishing ourselves each day on the Gospel. It is the solid rock on which we can base our hopes.

Why Luke wrote his Gospel

Dear families, from the four Gospels we have chosen that of Luke. I would like to say a few words to give you a general overview of the third Gospel. Luke was a disciple of Jesus who found himself in the same situation that we are, in the sense that he had not seen Jesus with his own eyes but had believed in him on the words of those who had known him. Thus, having let himself become involved with the faith, he did not want to keep for himself what he had heard and so decided to write what had struck him most so that others might be attracted to Jesus of Nazareth. He began to collect various materials and then to order them according to a plan that he had conceived. Students tell us that the third Gospel is the first part of a single work which Luke dedicated to Theophilus. In this first part he narrates the events surrounding Jesus, whereas in the second – the Acts of the Apostles – Luke tells of the events surrounding the apostles from Jerusalem to Rome. His intention is both historic and theological: he wants to show that Jesus has opened a universal way to salvation; a way that led from Jerusalem and ended up in Rome, the heart of the Empire and of the then-known world. Luke wants to show, by means of this work divided into two parts, that no one is foreign to the

Gospel, no one is unable to accept this news; no one is incapable of listening to it and accepting it. Everyone – even we today – can listen to it and be saved.

Luke never appears directly in his work (only Paul names him twice calling him my "dear doctor"). He knows well that it is the Lord who has to appear and to attract, not him. To write his Gospel he made use of three principal founts: first of all the Gospel of Mark (from which he has taken a large part of his narration), then from some sayings of Jesus, and finally from other traditions known directly by him, for example, the stories about the infancy of Jesus. Luke, after having collected all this material, profoundly reworked it giving to the evangelical account his own structure which makes it stand out with respect to the other three.

How did Luke tell the story of Jesus?

After a prologue in which he tells the reader of his intention to set forth the deeds of Jesus, the evangelist offers us the "Infancy Gospel." It is a matter of two chapters that are exclusively Luke's. In this regard a noted scholar states: "Perhaps we may never have known about the moving atmosphere surrounding the Birth or the wonder at the annunciation to Mary, if a Christian of the second generation had not told and elaborated on these records in the fabric of a work that goes only under the title of the Gospel according to Luke." In effect, these stories have nourished the liturgy of the nativity, the piety of the people, and Christian art itself for centuries.

The evangelist then follows with a brief section that introduces the period of the public life of Jesus (chapter 3) and this is followed by a long section where what Jesus said and the things that he did are recorded (chapter 4 to 19). In the first part (from chapters 4 to 9) the evangelist tells about the actions of Jesus in Galilee beginning with his well-known sermon in the synagogue of Nazareth where Jesus proclaimed a year of grace (a Jubilee), up to the transfiguration. From that moment the evangelist opens the central section of the book (chapter 10 to 19): this is the story of the long walk of Jesus to Jerusalem. It treats of a journey which is not only physical but also spiritual and which has to do with disciples of all times. All of us are on a journey toward Jerusalem, we toward that of heaven. As then, even today Jesus continues to teach the crowds about how to be his disciples, namely Christians. A characteristic of Luke is his emphasis on love for God and for one's neighbor which every disciple must have, and then the sense and the value of prayer in the life of the Christian before a God whose mercy knows no limits. For this reason many call his narration the "Gospel of Mercy."

With chapter 19 Jesus reaches Jerusalem: His preaching ministry continues with a long eschatological discourse (up to chapter 21). The final part of the Gospel (from chapter 22 to 23) describes the final events in the life of Jesus: his passion and death. It is a story that the evangelist integrates and modifies with respect to the other traditions in order to exhort the reader to conversion and hope. The scene of the death contrasts the "gospel of the world" (summed up in the common cry directed at Jesus from under the cross: Save yourself!), with the "Gospel of Jesus" who forgives everyone, including the thief crucified alongside him.

The final chapter (24) tells of Easter day. Luke alone tells how Jesus spent the entire day with two anonymous disciples who had become saddened by events and were returning from Jerusalem to Emmaus. He presents himself as a stranger and joins them. For the whole trip he opens their minds to the Scriptures and then, once inside the house, he opens their eyes when he breaks the bread. Listening to the Word of Jesus and participating in the holy meal is the way in which the disciples of all times meet the Risen Lord.

Read the Gospel every day in your family

Dear families, in this short volume I have divided the entire Gospel of Luke into 135 segments. The theme of each section is expressed in a title phrase, after which follows a brief spiritual comment. In this way, listening day after day to the Gospel passages, we will grow in our knowledge of Jesus. We will be pressed as it were to enter into his heart and into his days: we will follow him on his trips and participate in his compassion for everyone; we will take part in his gentle manner with the little ones and the weak; we will be moved by his ability to stand with the poor; we will weep at seeing how much he loved us; we will rejoice in his resurrection which definitively defeated evil. And we will also say: "He has done all things well." Who among men, in fact, ever lived with equal human and spiritual intensity as he did? If we read the Gospel in this way, we will certainly understand better who Jesus is. And knowing him, we will also know how to love him.

It is necessary to read one page of the Scriptures every day. Each day we are invaded by words, images, messages, invitations, etc. Not all are good messages since very few help us to live. Even at home there is the risk that for various reasons we don't always speak well and our words can do a lot of harm. We all feel the need for good words that touch the heart: the Gospel is the word that reaches into the heart. In the Our Father we ask God for our "daily bread." The words of Jesus are "living bread come down from heaven" offered to us each day. It is the very best bread: It nourishes both heart and body. Unfortunately many times we don't profit from it. And still it is given to us freely and in abundance.

Dear families, to read the Gospel together is one of the most beautiful and efficacious ways to pray. The Lord is especially pleased by this. Do you remember the episode between Martha and Mary? Jesus makes it a point to say to Martha, who was upset seeing Mary sitting and listening to him, that Mary had chosen "the better part," the part which is more needed. It is easy for all of us to be overwhelmed like Martha, by things that have to be done, by questions that have to be resolved, by problems to face, by difficulties to be handled. Mary – Jesus also says to us today – has chosen the better part (Lk 10:42).

Dear families, this little book wants to help making listening to the Gospel the "better part" of your day, the "better part" of all the days of the year.

We need to listen. The first step in Christian prayer is listening to Jesus who speaks to us. Yes, dear families, before multiplying our words directed to the Lord, let us listen to those which he directs to us. Every day. Let us try to listen to him and we will have the same experience that the two disciples on the road to Emmaus had, who felt their hearts burning within them and the need to remain with him. Listening thus was transformed into prayer and their meeting with Jesus threw new light on their lives.

How to read the Gospel every day

The present book time and again points out a passage from the Gospel of Luke followed by a brief spiritual comment which helps to tie the passage to our own life. This is decisive: the Gospel is addressed to us in order that we might be converted to the Lord and follow him. There is no need therefore to read it all in one sitting as we might some other book. No, the Gospel should be parceled out to us each day, a little like a mother breaks the bread so that her child can eat it without too much difficulty.

It's necessary to come together and to create a little zone of silence around us. We know how difficult it has become to find a moment of silence and prayer. But it is indispensable. We can say that daily prayer is our way of always praying, without ever getting tired. Yes, to pray every day with the Gospel is our way of praying always.

Hence we have to find a moment to be together, perhaps before a meal, or at the end of the day, or even at the beginning. Or at another time. What counts is to set aside five minutes to pray in a way that is brief but efficacious.

After the sign of the cross and a short invocation to the Holy Spirit that he might fill our hearts and enlighten our minds, someone could read a biblical phrase and then comment on it. At the end all could recite a prayer, perhaps the Our Father, and thank the Lord for the gift of his Word.

At the end of each passage I have added a particular thought that contains a suggestion to put into practice. Some families to whom I had given this book, in fact, recommended the inclusion of these exhortations or proposals. You could say therefore that this "work" was in a way "done in house," with families and for families.

Many saints have prayed in this way. St. Francis of Assisi, for example, had a great veneration for the Gospel. He read it at home, seeking to put it into practice to the letter, "without adding anything," as he liked to say. In the *Fonti Francescane* we read that "he used to write [...] a kind of *evangelario* or Service Book containing the Gospels and when, on account of sickness or other clear impediment, he could not attend Mass, he would read the passage assigned to the Mass of that day. And this he continued to do right up to his death. He gave this reason: 'When I don't attend Mass, I adore the Body of Christ in prayer with the eyes of my mind in the same way in which I adore it when I contemplate it during the Eucharistic celebration.' Once having listened to or read the evangelical passage, St. Francis, because of his great reverence toward the Lord, always kissed the book of the Gospel."

He, together with a long line of believers, literally understood the expression of Jesus: "Not by bread alone does man live, but by every word that comes forth from the mouth of God" (Mt 4:4).

Dear families, it is my wish that listening to the Gospel each day everyone will be helped to follow Jesus. We are all aware of our limits, of our weaknesses, but we also know that by listening to Jesus we will feel his companionship and his blessing every day.

A brief summary of how to reflect on the *Gospel of Luke* as a family with the help of this book

Agree on a regular time when all of the family can gather together to experience these four moments:

Listening

Read aloud the designated passage from the Gospel together with the commentary heading that highlights the central idea of the passage.

Reflecting

Use the brief commentary provided in this book to reflect for a moment on what the Lord wants to say to you. Share your reflection.

Praying

After listening and reflecting together, pray for whatever you wish. Conclude your petitions with the *Our Father*.

Acting

What is this Word asking of you? The small suggestion at the end of each section offers a challenge for your family life. You can take up this challenge or choose another that would be more significant for you.

A HOME FULL OF MERCY

1. The Gospel is good news that changes the world (Lk 1:1-4)

The Gospel is not the fruit of human reasoning or thinking; it is born from events that have been fulfilled among us, as Luke writes. It deals with the words and actions of Jesus of Nazareth. These "events" became Gospel, that is, good news for the whole world, even for us. The Gospel, therefore, is a living word that continues to speak to us: it is good news even for our time. And the good news is this: with Jesus the mercy of God has appeared in the life of men. The face of Jesus is the merciful face of the Father. Every generation is called to be confronted with this news, to listen to it again in order to draw from it strength, light, sustenance, and companionship. The evangelist, addressing himself to Theophilus, wants to entrust this news to him in order that it might be spread throughout the world. It has even reached us. And whoever loves the Lord or who seeks him with a sincere heart will find in it the radical response to the meaning of life. If we approach these pages with a sincere heart we will find the same power that emanated from direct contact with Jesus. We might even say that the Gospel makes us contemporaries of Jesus of Nazareth.

At the Dinner Table

What is the episode in the life of Jesus that you like the best? Why? Let each one tell the story.

2. The angel announces to Zechariah the birth of John the Baptist (Lk 1:5-25)

Luke's Gospel opens with the angel speaking to Zechariah in the temple announcing the birth of John the Baptist. Zechariah and Elizabeth are sterile. They have no children and, moreover, they are already quite old. We might say that the Gospel begins in a family and this one is marked by sterility. The two elderly parents ought not to have had descendants. Resigned to the inevitable, they no longer expected anything other than the conclusion of their own lives. The future was already marked without hope. In them we can see the life of many elderly people, resigned to spend the last days of their lives in a more or less sad state. But there are many such families that do not have children or who don't want to have them. God however intervenes with his Word and announces to Zechariah that his wife is going to have a son. "It's impossible; this is too much!" Zechariah thinks. And his incredulity causes him to become mute, no longer able to speak. The power and love of the Lord often clashes with our incredulity, with our resignation and we become speechless, that is without words of hope any more for ourselves or for others. Who does not listen and remains closed in on his or her own "ego" is unable to speak to others. The love of God, if we embrace it, conquers our incredulity and our sterility. And so it is that Elizabeth, in her old age, conceives a son: no one is ever so old as to no longer be able to see and to do new and beautiful things.

Between Grandparents and Grandchildren

Does the Lord still work today in the histories of persons? Perhaps the grandparents could recount some episodes in their own lives in which they especially relied on God and had seen the future bear fruit.

3. Mary, still a young girl, says her "Yes" to God and becomes the mother of Jesus (Lk 1:26-38)

Mary is a young girl like all the rest and lives the ordinary life of her village. And still the Lord's glance falls on her: she is chosen to be the mother of Jesus. One day an angel enters her home and she listens to what he has to say. Once again an angel enters a home. The beginning of this Gospel seems to favor the place proper to the family, the home. An ancient tradition would have Mary praying. It is in this moment that the angel appears to her. Why, then, not take care to find time to pray while you are at home? And how many are the opportunities to do so together! During her prayer the angel speaks. His is a very important message, such that Mary is disturbed in listening to what he has to say. The word of God, in fact, does not leave us indifferent. Mary, unlike Zechariah, aware of her own weakness, gives her consent to the good news. She takes it to heart. And from that day on, the history of the world changes: it has been more than two thousand years since "the Word became flesh." Mary, with her "Yes" becomes the first believer, the first to take to heart the word of God who thus became flesh of her flesh. Mary stands before us and continues to teach us the way of faith, which consists in listening to the good news. Together with Mary we too can respond to the angel: "Behold the servant of the Lord; may it be done to me according to your word."

Between Yes and No

With the yes's and no's that we pronounce each day, we make the world truer and more beautiful or sadder and darker. Let us decide together to what we want to say "Yes" to and to what we want to say "No."

4. The teenage Mary visits her elderly cousin Elizabeth (Lk 1:39-45)

Mary, after having learned from the angel that Elizabeth was pregnant, rushed at once to her side. She went in haste, Luke writes. The Gospel always makes people hurry, pushes them to leave their old habits, their own preoccupations and their own thoughts. And how many thoughts Mary must have had in those moments, after the word of God had completely turned her life upside down! The Gospel forces us to get out of ourselves and pushes us to leave our homes and our self-preoccupations to go in search of those who suffer or who are in need, like the elderly Elizabeth who was facing a difficult maternity. We might say that a young teenager went to visit an old lady. It is an example that many young people should imitate. Elizabeth, as soon as she sees the young Mary enter her house, rejoices profoundly in the depths of her being. It's the joy of an elderly person being visited by a young person. It is the joy of the weak and the poor when they are assisted by the servants of the Lord, by those who believed that the word of the Lord would be fulfilled. The word of God creates a new bond, a unique bond between the disciples of the Gospel and the poor, between the young and the old.

Someone is Waiting for Us

This page from the Gospel is for us: today a grandparent or someone near home, especially someone who is elderly and alone, is waiting for us. Let us not leave them alone!

5. Mary, full of joy, thanks the Lord with her *Magnificat* (Lk 1:46-56)

Mary appears right from the beginning marked by the beatitude of those who listen to the word of God. The first beatitude of the Gospel, as Luke writes, is addressed by Elizabeth to Mary: "Blessed are you who believed that what was spoken to you by the Lord would be fulfilled." In her hymn, the *Magnificat*, Mary expresses the happiness that she felt as a young girl. Mary, a poor teenager from a forgotten village on the outskirts of the Empire, sings out her joy because the Lord of heaven and earth looked down upon her in her lowliness. She did not think of herself as worthy of consideration nor does she claim anything for herself. She knows that everything comes from God and from God is his greatness and his power. This very same God who liberated Israel, who protected the poor, who humiliated the proud and who filled the hungry with good things, looked down on her and loved her. She, for her part, listened to him in her heart. And from that day on, through her, God took up his domain in the midst of men. Mary doesn't forget to sing of the mercy of God which reaches from generation to generation.

An Invitation to Mothers

Try to associate yourselves to the song of mother Elizabeth and mother Mary: today dedicate some minutes to thank the Lord for your children and for the joy they have brought into your life.

6. Zechariah also gives thanks
(Lk 1:57-80)

For Elizabeth the time had arrived for her to have her child and she gives birth to a little son. Not only are she and her husband Zechariah happy, but so too are their neighbors. Every time, in fact, that the word of God is embraced and bears fruit a new climate is created both in the family and in its surroundings. The Gospel always creates a new climate between people. Zechariah, having once again become a believer, regains his speech and praises the Lord. And, like Mary, even he cannot contain his joy and bursts into a song of happiness – the well-known *Benedictus* – for the infant John, who will go before the Lord to prepare his ways. Zechariah's joy can also be ours. We should reflect on this episode: a family – that of Zechariah and Elizabeth – after having believed and seen the fruit of their faith, becomes communicators of the greatness of God, of his benevolence and his mercy. And they witness with joy their faith in the Lord. This family becomes for all of us an example. The Lord moves beyond the sterility of this elderly couple, answers their prayer, and gives them a son. Those who pray and embrace the word of God in their own hearts are certainly visited by God and bear fruit. And can sing of the mercy of God.

An Invitation to Fathers

Often, for the good of the children, you may find yourself being very strict with them, reproaching or criticizing them. Today go out of your way to speak well of them, to say something positive to them about who they are and what they are doing. Say some nice things about your children.

7. Jesus is born in a stable on the outskirts of Bethlehem (Lk 1:1-20)

The scene of the birth of Jesus is described by the evangelist in a very simple way: Mary and Joseph are together with the baby whom they placed in a manger. In one sentence is summed up the mystery of that night which changed the course of history, dividing it into "before" and "after." And still it is only a matter of a baby in a manger. This is what the shepherds saw, nothing else. And still, Luke adds, they were full of joy. After having listened to the angels, they obeyed what the angels said to them and started off towards the grotto where they found the baby Jesus. They didn't see a baby born in self-sufficient palaces of egoism and avaricious riches. The little infant was born in a grotto on the outskirts of the city, and this because there was no room for them in the inn. How sad! In Bethlehem a door could not be found which would welcome that family of poor immigrants. It happens still today that so many poor, weak, tortured, refugees cannot find room in our cities and in our nations. We, like those shepherds, are asked to keep listening to the words of the angel: "A savior has been born for you […] you will find an infant wrapped in swaddling clothes." Let us get up and unite ourselves to them in their search: we too will see a baby and will rejoice in having found him who is our salvation. In that grotto, with Mary and Joseph together with the shepherds, we are able to perceive the first signs of the Christian community: all gathered around Jesus.

Faces

Search online for some images or actual stories of refugee or unwanted babies: do this not only to become indignant or simply to be saddened, but to perceive in the face of those babies some trace of the Son of God.

8. Simeon and Anna, two elderly people, welcome Jesus with Mary and Joseph in the temple (Lk 2:21-38)

Luke, in the first two chapters of his Gospel, introduces us to four elderly figures, first Zechariah and Elizabeth, and now Simeon and Anna. All four played an important role in the mystery of the birth of Jesus. It took place exactly contrary to how our society considers the elderly today. For contemporary society the elderly are to be set aside and, if necessary, pitied. In any case they are not always considered worthy of attention and respect. For the evangelist, instead, Zechariah and Elizabeth, in their old age, give birth to him who will prepare the way for Jesus. And Simeon and Anna welcome Jesus in the temple. The elderly Simeon – I should say in the name of all the elderly – takes him in his arms and intones one of the most moving canticles in the Gospels. Anna, with her 84 years, is also deeply moved in her heart by that baby about whom she becomes the first preacher. Yes, the Lord doesn't discard the elderly, does not distance himself from them. On the contrary, he gives them a new mission. It is certainly important even for the elderly to meet the Lord as happened with Simeon and Anna. From their encounter they were given new vigor, a new vocation, a more intense and more important life than before.

Together

The presence of God and his will is revealed in this meeting of the elderly, the adults, and little children. Why not try to pray simply, once, all together today? Just some traditional prayers, but united and in one voice!

9. The Family of Nazareth, thirty years of an ordinary life (Lk 2:39-40)

The story of the birth of Jesus ends with the arrival of the family of Mary, Joseph and Jesus in Nazareth. There are only two verses, but they cover thirty years, exemplary for every Christian family. The thirty years of the "hidden life" of Jesus in Nazareth are thirty years of very ordinary family life. Spoiled as we are by heroes and protagonists, we would like to ask: Why didn't Jesus initiate his public work immediately with signs and wonders? In truth he made himself like all of us so that it would appear that salvation is not estranged from the ordinary life of everyone. Yes, salvation comes by means of ordinary life in the family. There are no miracles in Nazareth; there are no visions or crowds that are noticed. Perhaps also because of this the Church has considered "apocryphal" all those stories created by the well-meaning curiosity of the early Christians who wanted to render extraordinary and miraculous the infancy and adolescence of Jesus. These two verses are a kind of synthesis of thirty years of an ordinary life, of a whole life, Jesus' and our own. That is to say, even we, in the very ordinary living out of our daily life, are asked to "grow and become strong, filled with wisdom" under the watchful eye of God as Jesus did. And we will grow to the extent that every day we go through the Gospel page after page trying to put it into practice.

Agenda at Hand

Today try to do extraordinarily well something that needs to be done. Tonight recount an event where this normality well lived had filled and made the day cheerful.

10. Mary and Joseph find Jesus, a 12 year-old boy, in the temple (Lk 2:41-50)

It's the feast of Passover and Jesus fulfills his first pilgrimage to the temple in Jerusalem. It is his first Passover and one of those moments in which he speaks clearly of belonging to the Father. Not even Mary and Joseph, those closest to him, understood. It will be the same at his last Passover when even Peter, his closest disciple, did not understand him and left him alone. "Why were you looking for me?" he said to his parents. Mary and Joseph were looking for him with great anxiety. Why wouldn't they be anxious without Jesus? We often, though far away from the Lord, find ourselves in blessed tranquility. Or so it seems more or less. Mary and Joseph teach us to be justly preoccupied not to lose the Lord. They began searching for him. And in the end they found him in the place of prayer. Jesus is to be found first of all in the Gospels, in prayer, in our brothers and sisters and in the poor because these are the Father's concerns. Every family has to overcome the temptation to think only of themselves, they have to avoid the risk of closing in on their own narrow horizons and even to consider their children private property. No. We are all challenged not to live for ourselves, but to participate in the loving design of God, to make the whole of humanity one great family.

Thinking of the Future

Who more than we are preoccupied with the future of our children? Certainly the Lord! If our children are still growing up, we pray that they find their vocation and respond to it generously. If they are already adults, we ask for them the gift of fidelity to God's plan.

11. Jesus is the heart of the family of Nazareth (Lk 2:51-52)

Jesus' family was an ordinary family. We are called to contemplate it. We would be moved to know the prayers that the three said each morning and evening; we would be edified in learning how Jesus as an adolescent confronted his first religious and civic duties and how as a young man he worked with Joseph; and then there was his zeal in listening to the Scriptures and praying the Psalms. How many mothers could learn from the preoccupation of Mary for her son! And how many fathers could take from the example of Joseph, that just man, who dedicated his life to providing for and defending not himself but rather the child and his mother! Still there is a depth to this family which remains hidden from our contemporary eyes, and which becomes unveiled for us by the Gospel: it is the "centrality" of Jesus. This is the "treasure" of the "hidden life": Mary and Joseph had welcomed this son, took care of him and watched him grow up in their midst, even in their hearts and their affection; and their understanding grew accordingly.

Selfies

The time is right to take a nice picture of the whole family and to send it to some relative or friend with a simple message of greeting. Help that person to perceive the treasure that you are, notwithstanding the rough edges and the fatigue that you deal with each day.

12. John goes to the outskirts… into the desert (Lk 3:1-6)

John is not just some man passing by. He is essentially a rough and rugged individual. He attracts us because we share with him the discovery of the true meaning of life, the answer to our waiting for the Lord, for salvation. He invites us to distance ourselves along with him from the city, from an intense life as a consumer of goods, of things, of affections, to seek a happiness that is always other than that. We have to retreat to the desert: to listen and to reflect. It is the word of God that drives John and us, to leave a sad past life and allow ourselves to be led by its light. The word of God – the evangelist notes – came to him in the fifteenth year of the reign of Tiberius Caesar. This tells us that the Word, the Gospel, is not an evanescent fact, an abstract and vague entity; nor is it a hidden and private voice. It is a word that affects everyone, the whole Empire. It descends into people's hearts and changes the life of the world.

Post-It

Among the messages stuck to the refrigerator put a nice colored post-it on which is written, possibly in large letters, a nice and important saying, a meaningful word in clear view in the kitchen each day. Who will be the first to suggest one at table?

13. John the Baptist pleads with us to be merciful (Lk 3:7-12)

John is preaching in the Judean desert outside of Jerusalem. His desert, however, is not far from us. Our cities, in fact, are often like an arid desert in life with an aridity that emanates from the scorching sun of egocentrism that leaves us prey to the "savage beasts" that devour the supernatural life of those who are weakest. John, a poor but free man, an austere and just man, speaks out vigorously and attacks the Pharisees and the Sadducees of all times, unmasking their ability to fake repentance and remain the same as ever. And he exhorts them to charity and generosity, to simplicity and to a life that is not unregulated and a prey to consumerism. But above all he wants them to make place for a new life in the populated and chaotic desert in which they live, to make way for the Lord Jesus, the only truly strong man who can "clear the air" of the anxiety, violence, war and nonsense that we find in this sad world of ours. He is the only one who can give us the Holy Spirit who inflames our hearts anew.

Put things in order

Today is a day in which to put your rooms in order, to learn how many things you own, which ones are useful, which are superfluous, and which you tend to waste.

14. In his Baptism Jesus is presented by the Father as his beloved Son (Lk 3:21-22)

Jesus, by this time in his thirties, leaves Nazareth and reaches the area of the Jordan River where John the Baptist is preaching and administering a baptism of repentance. Jesus leaves his place, home and family and joins this preacher. Arriving in the Judean desert where John is baptizing, he stands in line like all the rest to receive that baptism. And while Jesus is at prayer, the heavens open and a voice from heaven can be heard: "You are my beloved Son; in you I am well pleased." The sky, gloomy on account of the sins of men finally opens up, and from it descends a dove that rests upon Jesus as on its nest. From that moment on heaven is no longer closed. It is true that men, from time to time, have done violence to it with the sinister lightning flashes of war, the dark fumes of genocide, the pollution of the air and hearts. But the Holy Spirit breaks through every barrier and descends upon the disciples of that "beloved Son" every time that they welcome the Gospel and open themselves to love.

Family Album

Look at the photographs or videos of your baptism, and recall some anecdote regarding that day and explain why you were baptized with that name. Then light a candle (remembering the one we were given during the celebration), and pray together to the Father who has made you his children in Jesus.

15. Jesus enters the world of men
   (Lk 3:23-38)

At thirty Jesus leaves Nazareth and begins his public life (only Luke tells us the age of Jesus). For him it is a decisive moment: he begins his preaching on the streets and in the squares of his land. But it is also a decisive moment in the history of mankind: God no longer speaks through prophets but directly through his Son. And Jesus, under certain aspects, comes up against the longing of all the history which preceded him and takes upon himself the need that the world, the whole world, has of salvation. Jesus is not a magic figure of some kind. On the contrary he is truly one of us, with his own history, his own genealogy. The reading of this page from the Gospel might seem arid and without sense. In truth it tells us that Jesus is true man, our true brother. The evangelist collects the names of 72 generations, a sacred and perfect number representing all of history. Jesus is presented to us as a living word for all generations to come, our own included.

Waiting

   Tell your children about the expectations and preoccupations that you had while waiting for their arrival. And if you have a few minutes more to spend try to build a genealogical tree of your family. How far back are you able to go and to what generation?

16. Jesus conquers the temptations in the desert through the power of the Word of God (Lk 4:1-13)

After his baptism in the Jordan, Jesus is clear by now what the will of the Father for him is. And full of the Holy Spirit, he retires to the desert for a period of reflection and prayer. The desert, which in the Bible represents the obligatory passage in the liberation of the Jews from slavery in Egypt, welcomes the new Moses. Here Jesus has to confront temptations. He is in fact in every way similar to us, minus sin, as Paul says. The temptations that Jesus undergoes are three, but these represent all the temptations human beings face. There are first of all the typical temptations of the desert: when one is hungry, what could be more necessary than bread? This temptation is to consider the satisfaction of self as the primary purpose of life. Then there is the temptation of heights, we might say of the mountain top: namely to live in order to wield power over others, making use of them and not serving them. And finally there is the temptation of Jerusalem, of the pinnacle of the temple: not to accept the fatigue of daily conversion and to want God to be at our service. Jesus conquers the three temptations calling each time on the word of God. It is a great lesson for each one of us.

For the Parents

Try to give in to the "healthy temptation" to turn off the TV when it is about to transmit its usual programs. "Turn it off." The children will not be happy, but you will be helping them to take a step away from "mediocrity."

17. Jesus initiates his mission starting on the outskirts of Galilee (Lk 4:14-15)

Following his stay in the desert Jesus returns to Galilee and begins to speak. He doesn't begin with Judea and Jerusalem, the center of both the religious and political life of Israel, but rather on the outskirts of Galilee, an area that did not enjoy a good reputation, inhabited as it was by poor and abandoned people. Luke writes that Jesus moved under the power of the Holy Spirit, as if to emphasize that he was not acting on his own or by his own initiative. He is not a protagonist who wants to make a show of himself and cause others to speak about him. He did not come to do his own will but rather that of the Father. For this reason, his movements and his words created a new atmosphere, that of a feast which very quickly spread throughout the whole region. It is what happens also to those who follow him.

Among Brothers

Who knows whether your little brother has something to tell you? How would he describe a shelter? Or how does one divide by two? These are very important things to him. Today give him a little of your attention.

18. Jesus preaches in Nazareth and proclaims a year acceptable to the Lord (Lk 4:16-30)

Jesus presented himself in the synagogue of Nazareth. It was certainly not the first time that he went there; Luke emphasizes that it was his custom to attend. But this is the first time that he expresses himself in this way. After the reading of the passage from Isaiah in which there is the annunciation of the coming of the Messiah along with the narration of the works of liberation that he would accomplish, Jesus stands up and says: "Today this scripture passage is fulfilled in your hearing." The reaction of those present is initially one of wonder and amazement. But then they show themselves to be decidedly hostile, even wanting to kill him. What happened? The Nazarenes could not accept that one of their own whom they had known since he was a young boy and had seen grow up, could speak with authority about their life. Jesus was proclaiming a year of grace, that is the end of all oppression; and each one was to change his or her heart. The inhabitants of Nazareth rejected the idea that the Gospel might have authority over their lives. It happens even today to us whenever we refuse to listen to it.

Reserved for the Mothers

It may be that your adolescent sons and daughters are more inclined to listen to advice from their best friends rather than from you. There is not much you can do but you must not turn your back and say: "I can't do anything. Do as you please!" Our mission does not allow that.

19. Jesus is moved and frees a man from an evil spirit (Lk 4:31-37)

Jesus, thrown out of Nazareth, the city where he had lived, left for Capernaum, the most important center in the area. This city, in a certain sense unknown to him, becomes his new home. Even here Jesus, as is his custom, goes to the synagogue on the Sabbath. The evangelist notes that all were afraid because he taught with authority. His word is authoritative, direct, strong, and urges a change in lifestyle. In the synagogue there is a man possessed by an unclean spirit. Jesus approaches him and intervenes with authority. There takes place a kind of violent struggle between the evil spirit and Jesus, but it is Jesus who commands the evil spirit to go out of him and to leave that man free. And thus it happened. Thus begins the defeat of evil by means of the Gospel. This authoritative and strong Word Jesus gives to the disciples of all time, even to us, in order that in every city and nation we can banish the spirit of evil that enslaves men and women in order to give to everyone a new life, freer and more serene.

Human Respect?

At home, around the table set for a meal, to make a sign of the cross might be feasible. But in the pizzeria no; that would be too much; everyone would be looking at us! And what would they see? A Christian family who thanks God for a pleasant evening and for the good and hot sliced mozzarella!

20. Jesus heals Peter's elderly mother-in-law (Lk 4:38-39)

Jesus, having left the synagogue, enters the house of Peter. And here he is presented at once to the apostle's mother-in-law who is sick in bed. He bends over her, rebukes the fever, the evangelist writes, and heals the woman. The whole life of Jesus shows him bending over the poor, the weak, and in this case a mother-in-law. How many persons, most of all elderly, are today surrounded by indifference and by meanness and are constrained to remain in the sad situation of waiting for a solitary end! The Lord Jesus, bending over that woman, restores her strength to the point where she is able to get up and serve them. Jesus sets the example so that the disciples might continue to fight against all forms of marginalization. They should be the first to bend over others with love and to restore hope and life.

A Sweet Thought

A flower or a nice tasty sweet can be a nice thought for a special birthday: that of your grandparents. To be considered important by one's loved ones is the best medicine for everyone, small or big, young or old.

21. The poor and the sick knock at the door of the home of Jesus in Capernaum (Lk 4:40-41)

It is the end of the day and Jesus finds himself in the home of Peter in Capernaum. The evangelist notes that all those who have someone sick bring them to the door where he lives. The disciple's home, now the place where Jesus is staying, becomes the point of reference for the people of the city who bring their weak, poor and sick there. All knock at that door and stay out in front of it, certain to be heard. Should that not be true of every parish house? Shouldn't every Christian community be a true door of hope for those who seek comfort and aid? Should that not also be true for every believer? In the evening, at the end of the day, each one should recollect themselves in prayer and have before their eyes not only themselves or their own family members, but also the many poor and weak who, in every part of the earth, await consolation, friendship, healing and salvation. Our hearts too could become the door of that house in Capernaum where those who had need of help were gathered.

Attention to the Poor

On some Sundays parishes gather foodstuffs for the poor. Along with your little ones, take a sack of groceries for the poor with the intention of donating it to your parish food pantry.

22. Jesus preaches to everyone that the new world has begun, that of God (Lk 4:42-44)

It is dawn and Jesus retires to a solitary place, probably – as the evangelist often notes – to pray. This is an important and major teaching for each believer: to address prayer to the Lord at dawn means to orient one's day well. We, who often apply everything to ourselves, need to reorient our lives, our actions, our thoughts to God. And he will bless us "when we go out and when we come in" (cfr. Dt 28:6). A large crowd catches up to Jesus where he is found and try to hold him so that he won't leave. But Jesus emphasizes that he must announce the kingdom of God elsewhere as well. The good news of the kingdom, that is, of a world made of love and no longer violence, is not reserved for some people, nation, class, ethnic group or elite; it is for everyone. The Gospel, from the very beginning is seen as a universal message that supersedes every limit and boundary, precisely because the love of God itself is without limits, without boundaries.

Witnesses of Life

How do we help our children to have faith in tomorrow? By giving them a good motive, some "good news" by which to live. It will be easier if they could hear it from our lips, if they could live it through our actions, if they could see it in our eyes.

23. Jesus calls his first disciples and makes of them "fishers of men" (Lk 5:1-11)

Jesus speaks to the unruly crowd, tired and faint, looking like sheep without a shepherd. He was addressing not only yesterday's crowd, but also those of today who are likewise without anyone to care for them. Jesus wants to create around himself a small community of disciples who remain with him and help him in this work of mercy. He had a reason to get into the boat of Simon in order to speak to the people who remained on shore. Having finished speaking he asks Peter to put out into the deep and to lower his nets. They had fished all night without catching anything. But then, Jesus wasn't with them. And, without him, they could do nothing. Peter, all the same, listens to the command of Jesus and, though not understanding why, obeys. And an unprecedented catch of fish follows. It is so abundant that they have to ask others to help. Seeing this, Peter and his fishing companions left everything and followed Jesus. Thus the history of this remarkable fraternity that is the Church begins. The Gospel continues to call for new arms to enlarge the nets of mercy so that no one remains outside.

Workplace

At the time of Jesus to be a fisherman was the most popular kind of work. Today we have to thank God if we have a job. Let us take the Lord with us: Let's put a Christian password on our computer that reminds us to bless God, our work and our colleagues at the beginning of each day.

24. Jesus touches a leper and heals him
(Lk 5:12-16)

A leper, overcoming the difficulties of the crowd and the prohibitions of the law, throws himself at the feet of Jesus. He had already seen him earlier: the passing of Jesus creates a new atmosphere and bypasses prejudices and rules, often strongly held. So Jesus, bypassing every rule and tradition when he sees the leper, touches him with his hand. It is a gesture that breaks through the barrier that separates those who are healthy from the lepers, and above all it overcomes every fear. That hand which he stretches out does not represent a furtive gesture of courage; it is more like the guarantee of closeness, of a love that continues. One could say that it is the reflection of the love that Jesus has for the Father. Thus did Francis of Assisi do when he got down from his horse and kissed the leper: "What at first seemed repugnant, afterwards seemed sweet to me," he said, full of joy. The crowd ran to be close to Jesus and to listen to his word. But Jesus did not stop to enjoy the honor; rather he retires to pray. He knows that from the Father he receives all his power. If this is so for Jesus, how much more is it for us.

Bullying

How difficult it is to return to serenity after having been subjected to acts of bullying, even if only verbal, and to feel normal again! Learn to extend your hand, with love, to a companion who is being ridiculed, to a colleague being pointed at, to an isolated family.

25. Jesus heals a paralytic in body and soul (Lk 5:17-26)

Seeing their faith, Jesus heals the paralytic. The miracle was realized through the faith of that man's friends; a faith built on love, tenacity, perseverance and even the cleverness (opening up the roof) in order to bring their friend before Jesus. Notice what it is that brings about the alliance between believers (those who put their trust in Jesus and not in themselves) and the poor. They place the sick man in the center of the scene and not only physically. And Jesus, seeing their faith, seeing their love, immediately and completely heals that paralytic even more than anyone would have expected. Jesus, addressing the sick man, tells him: "Your sins have been forgiven." No one of those present had asked for this. If anything, the friends wanted the healing of the body and the Pharisees were only watching for this, not out of love for the sick man but in order to be able to discredit Jesus. But Jesus goes beyond the body and sees also into the heart of the paralytic, the need he had to be pardoned, welcomed and loved. And he gives him health of both body and heart. We could say that it is not by bread alone that the poor live but also by love.

Friendship

To live in Christ transforms our friends into brothers and sisters. Go through the numbers on your cell phone and with a text message say, "I was thinking of you" to some friend whom you have not heard from for at least a year. At a minimum you will have surprised him or her!

26. Jesus calls Levi, a tax collector, to follow him (Lk 5:27-32)

Once more Jesus leaves the house; he doesn't stay tied to a usual routine. He wants to go out in order to meet other persons and to announce the joy of the Gospel. Shouldn't that be the same for our parish which instead often remains closed in on itself, always with the same persons? Jesus took to the street and, while he was walking along, he met a tax collector by the name of Levi. This man is a public sinner, certainly considered by everyone as ill-suited for the Gospel. But for Jesus there is no one who is unsuitable, not even the greatest sinners. He calls and at once Levi, as did the first disciples, gets up and leaves his customs post and begins to follow Jesus. What counts is not the point where one finds himself but that he or she is open to listening to the call to follow the Gospel. Levi is no longer what he used to be; he wants his friends (publicans and sinners, whom everyone is obliged to avoid) to be able to meet Jesus as he had met him. And those, who like everyone felt the need to be loved, understood intuitively how precious is the love of the Lord who went in search of the poor and sinners. And how could they not have rejoiced in his company?

Making Reservations

Observe the many judgments you make of others today and how that affects your choices. Then promise to do better with the help of God.

27. The disciples have to celebrate when they are with Jesus (Lk 5:33-39)

Often we look for rules and regulations to follow, at times even severe, in order to flee the responsibility that the Lord asks of us in order to announce the Gospel. And so it was that the Pharisees praise the disciples of John the Baptist who fast and recite prayers, while they condemn the disciples of Jesus who instead throw a feast even outside of the time for feasting. But it is the celebration of those who have found the Savior of their own life; a feast so wonderful that the Gospel compares it to a wedding feast. Obviously even the disciples of Jesus will have to fast: to fast from their own egoism, from their own isolation, from their own stinginess, their own provincialism, in order to find themselves children of a God whom they will call "our Father." In fact they make up a part of a new family woven not with chains of flesh which restrict one, but with spiritual chains that open up the heart. They put on entirely new interior clothing, viz. that of the children of God, and their heart is like all the rest who have been newly filled to the brim with the new wine which is the love of the Lord.

Selfie

> *Publish on a social network a photo of the happy times that you have spent in the family, with friends, and colleagues, etc., because the Christian is a happy person, who knows how to value the joy of friendship, praying and fasting without letting it show.*

28. Jesus is Lord of the Sabbath and its rules
   (Lk 6:1-5)

On the Sabbath it was not permitted to collect and to eat the heads of grain. And the Pharisees, scrupulous when it came to the law but forgetful of the heart and life of the people, were quick to accuse Jesus because he broke the law by not respecting the Sabbath. Responding to them, Jesus quoted to his adversaries from the same Scriptures and recalled that David himself ate not only the heads of grain but all the bread offered to God whose consumption was prohibited by the law. The "day of rest" is an invitation to place ourselves totally at the disposition of the Lord. It is not a question of an exterior rite. The Lord asks us to rest from work both in order to be able to participate at the holy liturgy where we, so unlike others, are built up as a unique family of God, as well as for helping others to live, especially the poorest, the littlest and the sick, to celebrate the love of God, that is, the joy of being together as brothers and sisters.

A Picnic

After having attended Mass, organize a picnic with other family members (from grandparents to grandchildren), friends and neighbors (even non-believers or those of different beliefs), each one bringing something to share and prepare group games in which all can participate.

29. Jesus heals a man with a paralyzed hand (Lk 6:6-11)

The Gospel speaks of a man who can no longer work because his right hand is paralyzed. We are able to see in him all those who are excluded from work, not because they are sick but on account of the economic crisis. Jesus meets him on the Sabbath in the synagogue. The Pharisees, red-faced with narrow-mindedness, were looking for a miracle, not in order to rejoice in the healing but rather to accuse Jesus. They are like the modern Pharisees who don't put man at the center of work, but rather raw production. Jesus, with a sharp order as if to indicate the decisions that one must take in this case, says to the man: "Stretch our your hand!" And the man was found to be healed. We see here an echo of the words of God during the days of creation, when he spoke and the world little by little was created. On that Sabbath Jesus continues the work of creation by giving the man the strength to work. To give work today to the unemployed is, so to say, to heal many from sadness and desperation. Not only. Every time a person can work with dignity we can repeat, as at the creation: "God looked at everything he had made, and he found it very good." Only those who are blind at heart could be saddened by this.

Listen

Even if we are not able to directly offer work to those who need it, we mustn't remain indifferent. When we hear of some opportunity to work let us remember those who have turned to us, and then spread in our turn the news so that this sign from Providence does not fall on deaf ears.

30. Jesus chooses the twelve apostles to help him in his mission (Lk 6:12-16)

Jesus selects his closest collaborators, those who will help him in proclaiming the Gospel. The initiative begins with him, or better with the Father. Jesus, in fact, doesn't do anything without the Father. This is why he spends his nights in prayer. For Jesus, and hence for every Christian and every Christian community, prayer is at the origin of every choice, of every action. We might say that prayer is the first work that Jesus accomplishes, which is the basis for everything else. When day came, Jesus calls to himself those whom he wishes. And he calls each one by name. The community of believers in not an anonymous community; it is not made up of persons without a name, without love. The name, in fact, tells the story, the heart, and the life of each one. But there is more. In this call there is also a change of name, a change of lifestyle. Simon becomes Peter, that is, "rock," the foundation. Each one of the disciples receives his own new name, his own new responsibility. This awareness becomes an integral part of the Christian life, of our own spirituality.

Involvement

The Christian lives in community because the Gospel is communicated together. If you have never done it, seek out a parish group or a movement of Christian inspiration that fits in with your inclinations and allow yourself to get involved.

31. The crowd surrounds Jesus and presses against him (Lk 6:17-19)

Jesus with the group of Twelve just constituted, descends from the mountain and he finds himself at once before a huge crowd come from every part of the area. It is a normal and very usual scene in the Gospels. And it ought to be so for every Christian community, for every parish. All of us ought to see before us the crowds of this world and not only the people of our own neighborhood but also the crowds of our own city and even from farther away. Everyone ought to be kept before our eyes. All persons, in fact, make up the crowds that are tired, ill, needy and often forgotten. Seeing Jesus they press in on him and seek to touch him. A great strength, a great energy which changes lives, emanates from him, from his Gospel. Those who see us ought to perceive in us the strength of the life which comes from the Gospel and which our existence is meant to proclaim and witness to with concrete gestures of love and mercy.

Openness

Let us not close ourselves within the walls of our homes but let us open our doors to others, our neighbors, colleagues, those whom we meet in the supermarket, on the bus, ready to listen to their problems and to take them upon ourselves.

32. Jesus, with the Beatitudes, points the way to happiness (Lk 6:20-26)

At this point the evangelist inserts the grand discourse of Jesus which, unlike in Matthew's Gospel, is placed in an open field, almost as if to make it closer to ordinary life. And Jesus begins with the beatitudes. He has before his eyes an enormous gathering waiting for a word of truth from him. And Jesus does not hold back. He at once shows them the way to happiness. It is not the way to happiness that the world points to, a way that often shows itself to be fallacious and deceptive. Jesus doesn't waste words. Four are sufficient. Four beatitudes well set out and clear. He announces to the poor, to the hungry, to the downhearted and to those thirsty for justice that God has chosen to stand with them. His nearness and that of the disciples will be a sign and a cause for great joy. Those who up until now have been excluded from life will be the privileged, those preferred by God. To us who are believers is entrusted the very grave and challenging duty of making others feel the privileged love of God. On the other hand, with those four words, Jesus threatens sadness for the rich and the powerful. They who search for happiness only for themselves will be abandoned to a sad destiny in this world.

True Joy

Let us learn to recognize real happiness: it is not that which comes from success, from money, from power, but that which issues from little daily gestures and from reciprocal love.

33. Jesus asks his disciples to love others without any limits (Lk 6:27-38)

Jesus addresses those who are listening and speaks words which no one else has ever uttered: "Love you enemies and do good to those who hate you." These are very strange words in the culture of the world and therefore easily set aside. One could even say that they are beautiful words but certainly not very realistic. Still only in these words will the world be able to find salvation and the strength to stop all wars, in order to build peace and knit together the living of peoples as one. For Jesus there are no more enemies to hate and to fight against; for him – and hence for every disciple – there are only brothers and sisters to love, if occasionally to correct, but always to save. God treats every one with mercy and benevolence, even the ungrateful and those who are evildoers. And Jesus presents to the disciples of every age, including our own, notwithstanding our narrowness, an ideal that is as high as the sky: "Be merciful as your Father is merciful." It is not a moral exhortation but a style of life. On this our very salvation depends.

Between Spouses
We must remember to never end a day, if we have argued, without asking forgiveness. Make good every situation of conflict before it is too late. Then sleep serenely.

34. Jesus teaches his disciples the art of living well (Lk 6:39-45)

The Gospel helps us to live well. And it is not a word reserved only to a few; it is for everyone and it is for everyday life. When Jesus says: Be merciful... don't judge... don't condemn... pardon, he is not speaking in the abstract. He was the first to put these words into practice. They overturn the mentality of this world which is used to look at the splinter in the eye of another and to forget the plank in our own. This attitude not only makes us blind, it inexorably leads us into the ditch of division and violence. The wisdom of life is rooted in a heart newly nourished by the words of the Bible. For this reason true wisdom consists in welcoming the good seed of the "joyful news," the true treasure of our life. The heart that has welcomed it will, for that reason, become like a tree, rendered wholesome by the Gospel, which will not fail to bear good fruit.

Self-Criticism

Let's begin with ourselves and do some self-criticism: in doing so we will better understand others and we will be led to judge less. Who wants to start?

35. The words of Jesus are a solid foundation for life, as the rock is for a house (Lk 6:46-49)

Our passage closes the discourse on the beatitudes. The words spoken by Jesus are truly words to live and die for. They are not in fact empty and insignificant words; nor are they simply moralistic exhortations. They are the foundation of our lives, as necessary as the foundation of a house: they have to be solid so as to remain forever, insured against the pain of disaster. The evangelical words are therefore embraced and put into practice daily. Every day they must form the foundation of our life, of our thoughts, our decisions and our actions. Therefore it is not enough to listen to them once and think that is enough. Often it happens this way. While we may read the Gospel occasionally, in general we set it aside. And no one thinks that in doing so we cause much damage. Can one set aside the foundation of a house? The Gospel is a living foundation for the edifice of our daily life; it makes it strong against the floods of evil that batter us each day. With the word of God, Jesus in the desert resisted the assaults of the evil spirit.

Family

Make it a point every month to select a phrase from the Gospel upon which to meditate and with it to orient your actions with the desire to note the fruits of the lived word.

36. With a word Jesus heals the servant of the pagan centurion (Lk 7:1-10)

Having finished his discourse on the beatitudes, Jesus enters Capernaum wanting to bring the evangelical word inside the city of men. Here he comes across a Roman centurion, a pagan who, even though he is an oppressor, paid special attention to the Hebrews to the point of having built for them the synagogue of the city. His preoccupation for his slave, having contracted a serious illness, drives him to turn to Jesus. Two sentiments characterize this centurion: love for his servant (even though he was not his son he treated him as such) and his faith in Jesus. Here we are dealing with a faith so strong as to make him utter those words which all Christians even today echo during the Eucharistic liturgy: "Lord, I am not worthy that you should enter under my roof but only say the word and my servant shall be healed." This centurion, a pagan, becomes the image of a true believer, of one who believes that a single evangelical word would be sufficient to save his servant.

Along the Way

As Jesus walked along the streets of Capernaum, we also seek today to wander through the streets of our cities and countryside with a different outlook and, wherever we can, to perform little gestures of friendship or of aid towards our brothers and sisters.

37. Jesus restores the life of a young dead man (Lk 7:11-17)

A young man is dead. He is the only son of a widowed mother. Every strand of hope appears to have been definitively broken. Nothing is possible for the son or for the mother except to bury the one and accompany the other, consoling her in her sorrow. Nonetheless, that which is impossible for man is possible for God. Jesus, seeing that funeral procession, is moved with compassion for the widow who was accompanying her only son to the cemetery. He approaches her and tells her not to weep; then he takes the young man by the hand and says to him: "Young man. I tell you, arise!" And the young man gets up and begins to speak. Did the centurion not say: "Say only a word and my servant will be healed"? The Gospel word is always efficacious if listened to with the heart. It restores life, provides energy to those who have lost it, gives a new heart to those who have hearts of stone, and gives brothers and sisters to those who are alone. There are so many young people who today live without any hope for their future, who wait for someone to say to them: "Young person, I say to you, arise!" The Gospel helps us to hope and to work for these young people.

Young People

How many young people do you know around you who are sad and deprived of hope? Today it is up to you to approach a friend to give them courage and faith in the future.

38. Jesus answers John: the Messiah has come to help the poor (Lk 7:18-23)

John is in prison, and even from there, almost as a representative of the long line of others like him in the world, waits for the Messiah, the liberator. This man of justice never gave up hope; he never let himself fall asleep under the lax and superficial atmosphere of the world. He sends his followers to Jesus to ask him: "Are you the one who is to come or must we look for another?" John believes in the promises of God and, in his own way, wants to hasten them. The response of Jesus is clear: it recalls a passage from the prophet Isaiah – parts of which we discussed in his homily in Nazareth – where he describes what will happen upon the arrival of the Messiah: "The blind will see, the lame will walk, the lepers will be cleansed, the deaf will hear, the dead will arise, and the poor will have the good news proclaimed to them." John would have understood that this prophecy had been fulfilled. And so, even today these signs manifest the nearness of the kingdom of God. To serve the sick and the weak, to give sight to those who cannot see and strength to those who cannot walk, to announce the Gospel to the poor, give the most authentic and clearest response to the question of salvation present in hearts.

At Table

Let each one tell others the story of an experience of volunteering that had particularly touched their heart. And if no one has been involved, try to think of places where you might begin.

39. Jesus praises the Baptist who had prepared the way (Lk 7:24-30)

After the disciples of John the Baptist had left, Jesus began to speak to the crowds about this divine prophet: John is more than a prophet, because he has prepared the way for the Messiah. Every believer and the whole Christian community are a little like the Baptist: they are to prepare hearts to welcome the Lord Jesus. The disciple, in fact, doesn't live to speak about himself or of his own interests, nor to affirm his own ideas or convictions. The whole life of the disciple is at the service of the Gospel. He acts so that the Gospel may reach the ends of the earth, touch the hearts of men moving them to conversion. The disciples and the Christian community, small or large though they may be is not important, are asked to continue to point the world to Jesus and to say: "Behold the Lamb of God." It is necessary to proclaim this with words and with the witness of one's life, just as John did.

For the Parents

Your children are always looking for a word of praise or a special hug from you. Today is the right time to give them this gift of love.

40. Jesus accuses the lukewarm of loving only themselves (Lk 7:31-35)

Jesus's judgment on his own generation is harsh indeed. A little further on he will accuse them yet again: "O unbelieving and perverse generation, how much longer will I be with you and endure you?" (Lk 9:41). Peter, too, on leaving the Cenacle on the day of Pentecost, declares to those who are listening to him: "Save yourselves from this perverse generation" (Ac 2:40). It is not a matter of taking a pessimistic position, so much as it is to recognize the blindness that every generation has in recognizing the "signs of the times," that is the signs of God and of salvation written in the history of humankind. In general we are all so taken up in ourselves and in our egocentrism that we are unable to see anything other than that which concerns us. What Jesus says is emblematic: John, who does penance, is accused of having a demon, and he who eats and drinks is called a drunkard. In truth we also often fall into conduct which irritates others or we whine because we want to defend ourselves at all costs.

Positive Thinking

It is true: the world offers us harsh and sad realities but, instead of being sorry for ourselves, let us try to find something good that is happening around us.

41. Jesus pardons and praises the sinful woman who bathes his feet with perfume (Lk 7:36-50)

While Jesus was at table, having been invited by a Pharisee, a prostitute approached him; she knelt down beside him and, weeping, anointed his feet. The scene was undoubtedly extraordinary in every sense. One can only imagine the reaction of those present, given the customs of the time. It is a reaction not only of annoyance toward this woman who had entered the house uninvited and even interrupted the meal, but also one of a severe judgment against Jesus. He, in fact, not knowing who this woman was, allows her to continue. To sum things up, it seems that Jesus did not understand. In truth, it is those present who did not understand either the love of that woman and her desire to be forgiven, or much less the love of Jesus. Instead Jesus, who reads the secrets of the heart, welcomed and pardoned her; and to teach those present, yesterday and today, he tells the short parable of the two creditors. And then he points out their narrow-mindedness in contrast to the tenderness of that woman who has not ceased kissing his feet. And he adds: "Her many sins have been forgiven because she has shown great love." Love wipes out sins and changes one's life.

Forgiveness

While you are at table, talk about what forgiveness is; tell of a lived experience of having been forgiven or of having forgiven someone and share the feelings that you had at the time.

42. Jesus has a group of women who follow him (Lk 8:1-3)

The evangelist tells how Jesus continues walking the roads of Galilee accompanied by the Twelve and some women, teaching and performing signs of salvation such as exorcisms and healings. Everywhere Jesus leaves a sense of hope, of rejoicing, as an expectation of a new life is created among the people. Characteristic of this is the group of women who are with him. Some of them, Luke writes, had been cured of evil spirits and infirmities, and started following Jesus. They in every sense created a new community, to the point of placing at its service all their resources. It is important to emphasize this because it shows how Jesus was able to go beyond the traditions and customs of his time. It would have been unthinkable for an ordinary rabbi to allow women entrance into the circle of his disciples. Jesus, instead, associates them to his own mission, as we will see in later pages of the Gospel.

Women in the Home

Today is the day in which your wives, mothers, sisters and grandmothers should receive from you a word of esteem and affection for all their service in the family.

43. Jesus is the sower who sows the seed of the word in the hearts of man (Lk 8:4-15)

This is perhaps one of the most important of all the parables seeing that Jesus himself explains it, almost as if wishing to say that if you did not understand this parable you would not understand the others either. The first thing that stands out is the generosity of the sower in sowing the seed of the Word: he scatters it everywhere, even on the road, among the stones, hoping that it can find some piece of soil to which it can attach itself and grow. For Jesus, who is the first and true sower, there is no field which could not be fit to receive the Gospel. And the field is the life of each man and woman, of whatever culture and race they may belong. The word does not seek to divide people into categories such as bad soil and good soil. Each one of us, at times is like the rocky soil, at other time like the soil overgrown with thorns, at still other times we are like the good soil. It is up to us to open our hearts so that we can welcome the seed. The Lord always goes out early in the morning to sow the Gospel in our hearts. And he asks us therefore to accompany him in sowing everywhere so that the Gospel can be welcomed and bear fruit.

Seed

Take some seed and try planting it in a container with a little soil thinking about what the "good seed" of your moral character might cause to flourish even more.

44. Jesus pleads with us to show our faith
   (Lk 8:16-18)

Faith is never a private affair reserved to a little group. As light does not exist for itself but illuminates that which is around it, so the believer and every community of believers do not live for themselves but in order to manifest to everyone the Gospel. Jesus says: "No one who lights a lamp conceals it with a vessel or sets it under a bed; he places it on a lampstand so that those who enter may see the light." The Gospel has been given to us so that in our own time we can give it to the men and women of our city. Each parish, each believer, can therefore be compared to a lampstand: it must be placed up high in order to make the light of the "good news" shine. Obviously it is not a matter of showing off one's self, but rather to manifest the Lord. For this it is necessary above all to listen to the word of God; only the one who possesses it can give it to others and assist them on the way of salvation.

Light

   Light a little lamp or a candle. Each one should repeat a word among those spoken by Jesus which he or she considers particularly significant.

45. Jesus creates a new "family": his disciples (Lk 8:19-21)

Relatives of Jesus went to look for him, perhaps to extract him from the life that he had undertaken and which was creating not a little inconvenience. They found him surrounded by a lot of people and they were not able to get close to him. They ask one of those present to tell Jesus that his mother and brothers were waiting for him outside. It was not by mistake that the evangelist notes that they remain "outside" the group of those who were listening to him. Jesus responds that his true family is composed of those who were surrounding him listening to him. Those who are "outside," even if related to him, are not part of his family. The Gospel, in fact, creates a new family, not made by natural ties, but by those more solid ties which the Spirit creates. To be part of this family one thing alone is required: to listen to the Gospel, ponder it in your heart, and put it into practice. In fact this happened to Mary, the disciple of all disciples, who believed that the word of the angel to her would be fulfilled.

Friends

Speak to your family about a friend whom you sincerely love as a brother or sister and explain the reason for this beautiful friendship.

46. Jesus calms the waves that are buffeting the ship (Lk 8:22-25)

Jesus continues his ministry in Galilee, in the northern region. One day, when he found himself on the bank of the Lake of Tiberias, he got into a ship with the disciples and asked them to cross with him to the other bank. The preaching of the Gospel couldn't remain there where the disciples lived, on this familiar shore; there are other people who need to encounter Jesus and to listen to his word. The disciples therefore get into the ship with Jesus who, perhaps out of fatigue, went to sleep. And behold an unexpected storm came up and battered so hard against the ship that the very lives of the disciples were placed in danger. It's a scene that recalls many similar situations in our own lives. The disciples are agitated and fearful. Jesus, instead, is sound asleep. The disciples wake him up and Jesus begins immediately to bring calm to the lake. Those who remain with the Lord and call upon him in prayer will never be defeated; the forces of evil, which till now seemed to prevail like the winds of a storm, will be constrained to keep still.

Who is Sleeping?

At times don't we think that Jesus is asleep; are we sure that we are not the ones who are "asleep" forgetting that he never denies us his help?

47. Jesus combats and defeats the devils that enslave men (Lk 8:26-39)

After having calmed the tempest on the lake, Jesus reaches the other bank. It is pagan territory. We are dealing here with a symbolic landing place: the proclamation of the love of God is for every man and woman. As soon as they arrived on shore, a man possessed by demons, oppressed that is by evil and by the many slaveries of this world ("legion" evokes the multitude of demons present) approaches Jesus. The man no longer lives in the city. He remains outside, on the margins of life. Jesus, after a short exchange with the demons, as if to emphasize that a battle is going on, expels them, ordering them into a herd of swine who rushed down the steep bank into the lake. The people were seized with fear on account of all this and ask Jesus to leave there. Evidently their shock at these prodigious signs was not enough. It was necessary to convert their hearts. The cured man, instead, was told to stay with his people and witness to the power of the Gospel.

Witness

Jesus is a "living message" for everyone, good and bad, prophets and "demons." Are we sure that we understand him always and are able to "explain" his "message" to our neighbor with our comportment?

48. Jesus heals a sick woman who touches the hem of his garment (Lk 8:43-48)

Afflicted for years by a serious hemorrhage, this woman sees her life being diminished day by day by the violence of her sickness which seems unstoppable. She had knocked on countless doors to ask for help, understanding, affection, friendship and for at least a little relief from her solitude and anguish. But she had found no one who would give her a hearing and a remedy. It is the story of many misunderstood requests; the story of many women taken advantage of and not loved. This woman of the Gospel who has no name represents all of them. She thinks that Jesus is the only one who could heal her. She thinks that it would be enough just to touch the hem of his cloak. She hides herself in the large crowd, touches the hem of Jesus's cloak, and is healed. The disciples don't understand what is going on, while between Jesus and that woman an intense dialogue, full of love and faith, is taking place. Each one of us, every Christian community, can and must be like the hem of the cloak of Jesus that can be touched by whoever has need of our assistance, love and healing.

Counter-Currents

Even when the well-intentioned are certain of their judgment and firm in their pessimism, will we always be able to remember that Jesus is for everyone?

49. Jesus restores the life of a dead child
   (Lk 8:49-56)

Jesus, responding to the prayer of Jairus, head of the synagogue in Capernaum, resumes his walk to reach Jairus's gravely ill daughter. During their trip, however, servants of Jairus arrive to tell him not to disturb Jesus any further because his daughter is dead. Jesus, who had seen the faith of that man, exhorts him not to lose hope. The disbelief is general, both on the part of the servants and on the part of the people. Only Jairus continues to have faith in Jesus. Accompanied by three disciples, Jesus enters the house, takes the little girl of twelve years by the hand and restores her life saying to her "Arise." It is the same word used to describe the resurrection of Jesus. Even our children need to be taken by the hand in order to grow in the school of the Gospel and not that of the violence and egoism which leads to sadness when not to death.

Life

   Pay attention today to the negative affirmations that fill our discourses and substitute for them some positive messages of hope.

50. Jesus sends the Twelve out on mission (Lk 9:1-9)

Jesus had just healed an adult woman and restored life to a young girl. It is the battle between the evil that wants to dominate the world and Jesus who had come to liberate and to heal the world. Thus, even the disciples are mandated to fight this battle with the same authority and the same power of Jesus. He chooses twelve of them and gives them the power to cast out demons and to cure illnesses. It is Jesus who sends them out. It is the second time that the evangelist tells this story. The proclamation of the Gospel is not done once and for ever, nor is it an autonomous and private undertaking. Every disciple is called to insert himself in the long list of followers of Jesus to fight the same battle, to proclaim the same Gospel. For this it is necessary to get rid of our own ways and our own advocacy in order to bear the "good news." There is in this page a sense of urgency that causes the disciple to go from house to house, from village to village, from city to city, so that no one remains deprived of the evangelical message. Even Herod is curious. There will come for him the moment of encounter, but he will close his heart.

Apostles

Let us strive today to live one of the missionary dimensions entrusted to the twelve, feeling that we, like them, are "apostles."

51. The joy of the apostles over the fruits of their first mission (Lk 9:10-17)

The apostles return from their mission and Jesus takes them to a place apart where, however, they are soon reached by the crowds. Jesus, seeing those needy persons, is moved; he welcomes them and spends the whole day with them. Once evening had come, the disciples, thinking themselves to be more concerned than Jesus, suggest to him that he send the people to their homes for supper. But Jesus invites them to give the people a meal themselves. The disciples already having more than enough to do emphasize that they had only five loaves of bread and two fish, nothing with respect to the five thousand persons present. Jesus takes the little that they have and multiplies it for everyone. The miracle of the multiplication of the bread continues even today every time the disciples place in the hands of the Lord the little that they have and trust themselves totally to him. They will be the ones to distribute it but it is the Lord who does the multiplication. It is not a matter of being solitary heroes who do it all: it is enough to be servants of the Gospel who trust in the Lord and he multiplies life for everyone.

Shared Bread

Today make a little gesture requiring attention and sharing, trusting in the Lord: a little will become much!

52. The disciples of Jesus are called to give their lives for others (Lk 9:18-27)

Jesus frequently takes the disciples apart with him to pray. He is the image of the Christian community that gathers to pray in common. These were indispensable moments of intimacy of Jesus with his disciples. In one of these moments Jesus asks what the people think of him and who do the disciples think he is. Peter, in the name of them all, responds that he sees in him the Messiah. Jesus continues by announcing, for the first time, his passion, death and resurrection. The Messiah is not a powerful man according to the world's assessment. He came to give life. To follow him requires a "pruning" of one's ego, love for self and its practices. It is necessary to deny one's self and to take up one's cross. This is the way to true riches. Salvation doesn't consist in having a lot of consumer goods but in being bighearted and passionate for the Gospel.

The Cross

Let us pause for several moments today before the Cross and try to express what it evokes in us.

53. Jesus is transfigured on the mountain (Lk 9:28-3)

Eight days later, Jesus goes up the mountain with his three beloved disciples and is transfigured before them. The passage brings to a kind of conclusion the acts of Jesus in Galilee: in it he manifests himself to his disciples before beginning his journey toward Jerusalem. While Jesus is praying, the evangelist writes, his face is transformed and his clothing becomes dazzlingly white. We might say that this is what happens to the Christian community every time it gathers in prayer, above all for the holy Eucharistic liturgy each Sunday. Each one of us ought to say, as Peter did: "It is good for us to be here," to be with the Lord and with our brothers and sisters. The presence of Moses and Elijah who are talking with Jesus is meant to indicate the indispensable dialogue of the disciple with the Scriptures, a dialogue which conquers the sleep of egoism and permits one to listen to the voice from on high, a voice which opens the eyes and the heart to recognize Jesus as our savior and the savior of the world.

Scripture

Search in the Old Testament for some pages which help you to understand that they are speaking of Jesus and read them together as if Elijah and Moses were here in your midst.

54. Jesus heals a boy with epilepsy
(Lk 9:37-43)

Following the transfiguration, Jesus descends the mountain with his disciples and resumes his journey as usual. We might compare the scene with taking up our daily work after a Sunday pause. Jesus is at once surrounded by a crowd. There is among them a father who, shouting towards Jesus, pleads for the healing of his son, possessed and seized by an evil spirit. We can perceive in this the condition of so many young people who are slaves of consumerism and a life without meaning that dominates our "incredulous and perverse" society. Jesus asks that the young man be brought to him, as we seek to bring the Gospel to young people even today in order that they too, might be protected from evil incidents. It is significant that the disciples are not able to heal that young man: without the Lord, they were unable to do anything.

Young People

   Try to confront some young people today regarding an evil present in the world and how to combat it with the help of our Christian faith.

55. Jesus announces his passion to the disciples but they don't understand (Lk 9:43-45)

Euphoria regarding the evil overcome risks distorting the vision of Jesus. For this reason he calls his disciples to himself and, for a second time, predicts his death. Pay attention, Jesus emphasizes, seeking to break through their hardness in understanding him. The distance between the thinking of the disciples and the thoughts of the Master, a distance created by their self-sufficiency, deeply rooted in their tradition and unshakable convictions, is also ours. What happened to the disciples also happens to us: they didn't understand. It is not a question of words obviously but of the substance itself of the mission of Jesus: his death for the salvation of all. How can a defeated Messiah be accepted? And still it is out of the defeat of the cross that our salvation is born. The disciples are also saddened by not having understood. However what counts are not the states of their souls, but the effort and joy of understanding the heart and thought of Jesus.

Reflecting

Ask yourselves how you react to the mystery of suffering, death, or the unexpected occurrences that turn your plans upside down, and try to speak about this together.

56. The greatest of those near Jesus are those who serve others (Lk 9:46-50)

Why didn't the disciples understand the prediction Jesus made regarding his death? We may be able to find the answer in the initial phrase of this passage: They, in fact, were discussing among themselves who might be the first among them, a discussion which shows how distant they were from the Master. They were fully sons of this world and of the mentality which rules relationships between persons. But Jesus has turned the criteria of the world upside down. And so that the disciples might understand well, he takes a little child and sets it in their midst, almost as if to identify it with himself: "The one who is least among all of you is the one who is the greatest." In the kingdom of heaven the one who makes himself little is the greatest, the one who recognizes his own weakness and trusts entirely on the Lord. To John, and to all of us, Jesus says: "Who is not against you is for you." It is a great lesson in evangelical tolerance.

Lessons from Listening
   Today try to truly listen, giving space and attention to those who are familiar to us when they address us.

57. Jesus begins his journey to Jerusalem (Lk 9:51-56)

L uke begins this passage with the start of the journey of Jesus with his disciples to Jerusalem. Up till now he remained in Galilee; but he knew that the Gospel also had to be taken elsewhere, Jerusalem included. The disciples would have liked to stop him but Jesus resolutely – thus the evangelist notes – set out toward the holy city. He doesn't stay in places where he was known and secure. The Gospel, in fact, does not support boundaries and provincialism, even if this implies difficulties and opposition. From the beginning, Jesus encounters difficulties and lack of acceptance, but obedience to the Father and the urgency of the Gospel did not stop him, nor did it make him change the primacy of benevolence and love. Love even for those who rejected him. For this reason he criticizes the violent "zeal" of the disciples who wanted to destroy the Samaritan village which did not welcome them: for Jesus there were no enemies much less persons to be destroyed.

Tensions

Is there anyone with whom you live in some kind of tension? Entrust that person to the Lord today, asking that he or she be blessed by God.

58. The disciple is called first of all to follow Jesus (Lk 9:57-62)

Jesus had hardly begun his trip towards Jerusalem when right away the problem of followers was posed: how is one to follow Jesus? The examples that the Gospel report show the demands of the call. It is unusual that the three responses that Jesus gives to this matter regard the family in some way: in the first case the disciple is invited to recall that Jesus is often without a house and even a place where he can lay down his head; in the second Jesus affirms the primacy of the proclamation of the Gospel over the most delicate traditions of the family, as for example funeral rites; in the third he exhorts the disciple not to have regrets. In other words following the Gospel requires one to leave one's self and his or her own habits in order to choose Jesus as the sole Lord of his or her life.

Religious Study

    Actively take part in the hour for religious studies at school, making of it a time for personal growth and seek to involve a companion in it.

59. Jesus sends seventy-two disciples on a mission (Lk 10:1-16)

Seventy-two disciples are chosen to go into the towns where Jesus is about to visit in order to prepare the people for their meeting with him. They are not called to remain in these places forever. The Lord sends them so that they can prepare the men and women with the preaching of the Gospel to welcome the kingdom. St. Gregory the Great makes this beautiful observation according to which Jesus sends the disciples two by two so that their initial preaching might be that of mutual love. Love, in fact, is the power behind the work of the disciples of yesterday and today. The love of the Lord conquers the "wolves" of this world like the one that St. Francis confronted in Gubbio. The disciples were to take nothing with them except the Gospel and their love for the Lord. With this baggage we can travel the roads of the world even today, not witnessing to ourselves, or our customs, or our convictions, but to "him who has sent us."

Mission

It would be nice to invite a missionary home and to hear from his own lips the living experiences he has had and the way in which he felt himself accompanied by the Lord.

60. The real joy of the disciples is to be with Jesus (Lk 10:17-24)

The disciples experienced the irresistible power of the Gospel and the love that Jesus gave them. That evening, when they gathered around him, they were full of joy in telling about the prodigies of which they had been witnesses. Jesus rejoices with them: "I saw Satan fall from the sky like lightning." It is the joy that is born every time evil suffers a setback, defeated by the Gospel. Jesus confirms to his disciples the power and the protection that he had conferred on them. But he also made them understand that the secret of their life consists in having their own names written in heaven, that is, in the very heart of God. Communion with Jesus, with the Father, and with the Holy Spirit is the life of the disciple. Jesus thanks the Father because he has chosen to confide his secret of love to little ones. In this familiarity is contained our happiness and our blessedness as disciples.

Pause

How many times do you get together to pray? Try to find a special time during the day in which you stop, put aside your cell phones, turn off the TV and read a passage from the Gospel.

61. With the parable of the Good Samaritan Jesus shows the way for the Church (Lk 10:25-37)

This parable is among the best known pages of the Gospel. It describes well the situation of this world and it clearly shows the vocation of the Christian community and of every disciple. A man half dead left at the side of the road represents all the poor (individual persons but likewise entire peoples) still today set aside and left on the margins of life. It is a matter of millions and millions of persons. The Gospel teaches us to see that man as a brother of the Lord and as our friend. Yes, all those disinherited of the earth are brothers of the Lord; they are brothers of each one of us. The Gospel teaches us to "globalize" our brotherhood beginning with the poor. The Samaritan is Jesus himself; he it is who walks the roads from Jerusalem toward the many Jerichos of this world. He is the first one to halt, teaching all his disciples to do likewise. And, like the Samaritan, he does not stop with a single gesture, but surrounds that man with care and concern until he is healed. The world has need of a Church like this, of Christians like this; the poor above all have need of these.

Grandparents and Grandchildren

How many times have you called your grandparents on the phone, asking them how they are and if they have need of a little help? How many times, instead, are we the ones to ask them for something without giving anything back in return?

62. To remain at the feet of Jesus is the better part of life (Lk 10:38-42)

To remain at the feet of the Lord like Mary is the image of each disciple. The Christian, in fact, is above all one who listens to the word of the Master and keeps it in his or her own heart. The disciple resembles Mary more than Martha, who allows herself to be overtaken by an activism that upsets her to the point of criticizing even Jesus. The Christian can be an activist, a doer, a protagonist, but above all he or she is a disciple of the Lord. From listening to the word of God, in fact, arises all Christian being and acting; in prayer we discover that we are his children, able that is to say "you" to God and to trust in him with full faith. Because of this one could say that prayer is the first and fundamental work of the Christian; and that is true whether our prayer is personal which we can say anywhere or that which we recite in common. And, it is in prayer that we learn to love the Lord, our brothers and sisters and the poor. Love in fact is not born of us, of our character or our nature. Love is a gift of the Spirit that is poured out in our hearts when we place ourselves before God.

Surpluses

Let's try a little exercise together: on a piece of paper to be left in the kitchen write three things, situations, works that you consider superfluous and three that are essential and important in the course of a day. Then discuss them.

63. The "Our Father," the prayer which Jesus left us (Lk 11:1-4)

The evangelist tells us more than once how Jesus went off alone to pray. He wants to emphasize an essential dimension of his life and hence also in that of his followers. The disciples, in effect, observe their master at prayer attentively. In the end, one of them asks him: "Lord, teach us how to pray." It is a petition that we must make our own. We need in fact to learn how to pray, and to pray as Jesus prayed, with the same faith and confidence that he had towards his Father. The first word that he places on his lips is Abba, the tender name with which little babies address their fathers. And at once he clarifies that God is the Father of us all, our Father in truth. In the prayer the first thing asked for is to be recognized as children, babies who trust totally in our common Father. Praise then follows (holy be your name), the request for the kingdom (your kingdom come) and then to ask for bread and mutual forgiveness, two important dimensions of our life.

Space for Fathers

Today let us make space for fathers: let them emphasize, in whatever way they think most opportune, how Jesus is always close to their children as they are every day. Children, turn to God every day and entrust all your preoccupations to him; he will listen and know how to advise you.

64. Jesus assures us that prayer is always efficacious (Lk 11:5-13)

Jesus knows the doubts that the disciples have regarding the efficacy of prayer. And he wants to clear things up at once, so important is this for believers. He does so with two parables. The first is that of the troublesome friend, icon of the disciples who are invited to make themselves "nuisances" with the Father and to persevere in asking: "ask and you will receive." Insistent prayer forces God to "get up" and to fulfill requests. The second parable emphasizes that God not only responds, but gives good things to his children: he always listens. In a few lines the full force of prayer emerges, capable of moving God. The problem is that often we are not persevering, above all in prayer recited together, and in not a few cases do we find our faith truly limited.

Space for the Children

What are we asking God for today? He gives good things to his children. Let us leave the word to the children.

65. Jesus overcomes the mutism of those who do not know how to speak well (Lk 11:14-26)

Once again Jesus pits himself against evil, against that evil principle which enslaves a man, making him mute, incapable of communicating with others. All who were present, the instant they heard the man speak, marveled. But the evil spirit was not resigned and further strengthened some of the crowd in their resistance and opposition to Jesus and the Gospel. It is a story of great actuality: the inability to communicate is truly frequent, between persons, between relatives at times, among peoples and among nations. And the inability to communicate creates all kinds of tensions and conflicts. The evil principle wants divisions and animosities to increase. The disciples are invited to be attentive and watchful and keep up their guard so as not to be defeated by the evil spirits. Jesus is stronger and he alone can guard the "house" of which the Gospel speaks, namely, the heart of the Christian community. Only the one who is Lord can gather the fruits of love and hope.

Silence

Think back over the past week and try to ask yourselves: have we seen examples of mutism and of difficulty to communicate? Why? Then ask the Lord to guard you from forms of isolation.

66. Jesus, greater than Jonah, came to save the city (Lk 11:27-36)

This evangelical passage opens with the true blessedness of the disciple: "Blessed are those who hear the word of God and keep it." The first person to have lived this beatitude is Mary. She, in fact, was the first to welcome, keep and put into practice the word of God, the true foundation of the life of the disciples and for their being able to live together as men. So many today are looking for prodigious or miraculous signs to consolidate their faith and give them peace of mind. The great cities of today, like the great Nineveh, make life difficult, above all for the poorest of the poor. These are often the victims of physical and mental ostracism, created by poverty and marginalization, desperation and anxiety. For this reason so very many are looking for something prodigious in which to place their trust. In truth, there is need for the streets and squares of our cities to be crossed once again by the preaching of the Gospel, as happened when Jonah preached repentance to the Ninevites. The Gospel is far more precious than the wisdom of Solomon and far more powerful than the preaching of Jonah. For this reason the word of God cannot remain hidden but must shine forth and be a light to men. Christians must be the lanterns.

Lights

This evening light a candle and put in the window facing the street. Let it be a little testimony of your desire to be the "light of the world."

67. Jesus exhorts us to have a heart rich in mercy (Lk 11:37-44)

Jesus, invited to the house of a Pharisee, did not fulfill the ritual prescriptions required before a meal. This behavior occasioned a severe judgment. Jesus, aware of this, responds to the Pharisee by posing the question on another level, that of the heart. He clarifies that in life appearances don't count but being persons of a merciful heart does. If the heart is full of wickedness one's actions will be the same. For this reason, instead of condemning an action, Jesus wants to delve deeper. What counts is what each one has in his or her heart. Ritual observance has no value if one then violates justice and is far from love. Jesus exhorts us saying, "as to what is within, give alms," that is, give to the world the love which was poured out in your hearts. The disciple's wealth, therefore, does not depend on the multiplicity of rites that a person fulfills but in the fact of having a merciful heart.

Appearances

Let us teach not to stop at appearances. Before an individual who asks for alms, do not limit yourselves to giving a few small coins: also offer a smile, ask his name, stop for a while, without letting yourselves be conditioned by the fact that he has the appearance of a beggar.

68. Jesus encourages the doctors of the law to listen to the Word of God with humility (Lk 11:45-54)

A doctor of the law, listening to the harsh words of Jesus against pharisaical ritualism, says that in talking this way he offends not only him but all of his colleagues as well. With this reaction, he shows that he had listened to Jesus, but he did so with the pride of one who had to defend his own position. The word of God, as St. Paul says, is like a two-edged sword that penetrates to the heart and does not leave one indifferent. But if it is heard with pride and self-sufficiency, it becomes received as a reprimand that offends and not as a salutary and good force that changes hearts. If one remains a slave to his or her own pride it is easy to mistreat the prophets and the just; it is easy that is to eliminate their voice, forget their words and in every case distance them because they disturb us. We try to silence them and even build them beautiful tombs where they can speak no more. The "key" to entering into Scripture and into life is humble and docile listening.

Reporting

Listen and speak more to each other at home and in the family in order to learn to know and to respect each other more. Avoid the useless and gloomy words of those who are used to listening only to themselves.

69. Jesus speaks to the people and exhorts everyone to witness to the Gospel of love (Lk 12:1-12)

Many people gathered around Jesus; there were so many, Luke writes, that they "were trampling one another underfoot." All of those who were crowding around him had great need of comfort and hope and in Jesus they found an answer. Not so the Pharisees who, satisfied with themselves, refused to recognize in Jesus any authority over their lives. They were convinced that they had no need of him. Jesus warns the disciples and the crowd against this pharisaical spirit of self-sufficiency. The Gospel is for everyone; it therefore must be preached from the rooftops, even if this might cause rejection and opposition. Jesus has already experienced this himself; and he cautions the disciples that things will not go differently for them. They should not lose courage or fear those who can kill the body but not the heart. Those who can kill the heart are to be fled from because, taking the soul out of the Gospel, they take away the meaning of life. The Lord, who is the father of life, will defend his children and not permit that one of them be lost. This is the inheritance that many believers have left us (for example Christians martyred for their faith) because we too live through a love that knows no limits.

The Gift

Attach to the door of your refrigerator the name of some country at war to recall together the value of peace and to entrust these people to the Lord. In large letters at the end write the words "Thank you, Lord, for...."

70. Jesus condemns the man who accumulates riches only for himself (Lk 12:13-21)

Jesus then begins to show what the attitude of the disciple ought to be with respect to the goods of the earth. The occasion was offered by a man who asked Jesus to intervene and make his brother divide equally with him the property they had inherited. But Jesus refuses to intervene. He is not the master of division. He is the master of the word of God. He intervenes therefore not in the inheritances but in the hearts of men. It is in the hearts of the brothers where the problem hides, not in things. The hearts of the two brothers are weighted down with the desire for riches and are subjected to avarice; it is in this terrain where divisions and fights take root. Paul writes to Timothy: "The love of money is the root of all evil" (1 Tm 6:9-10). And Jesus explains this with the parable of the rich fool. This rich man believes that happiness exists in accumulating the goods of the earth. In his life – according to the logic of the avaricious person – there is no space for others, because life consists in accumulating goods exclusively for one's self. The rich man however has forgotten that no one is master of his own life. And happiness does not reside in the possession of goods but rather in love of God and of one's brothers and sisters.

Detachment

Make a gesture of detachment. Every day: give something that was given to you to someone else, something that you like very much, a moment that you wanted all to yourself. Be detached from the place, from the gift, and from its division.

71. Jesus exhorts us to place our faith in God who is kind and merciful (Lk 12:22-34)

Jesus continues to exhort his disciples not to be preoccupied with their life, with what they will eat or how they will clothe themselves. The Lord knows well that these things are necessary. One's life is more valuable than food and the body than what it wears. Jesus invites the disciple to look at the birds of the air and the flowers of the field: they have food and clothing in abundance. How much more then will men have! What is necessary will be given to the disciples. They don't therefore have to be slaves to worry over these things or to be obsessed with having. The first preoccupation of the disciple ought to be the search for the kingdom of God and his righteousness and the rest will be given them besides. This trust in God on the part of the disciples enlarges their hearts: the poor will be aided, the weak will be defended, and the ill will be visited. There will be none among them in need, Luke writes in the Acts (4:34), because the love of God will push them to be interested in the well-being of others. If our treasure is to be found in the persons that the Lord has given us, there also will our heart, that is, our love be.

Prayer

Thank the Lord for the gifts given to your family and pray for those who are alone.

72. Jesus asks us to be vigilant and not to be resigned (Lk 12:35-48)

To the rich fool surprised by death, Jesus compares the disciple awaiting his Lord. Vigilance is one of the spiritual dimensions of the Christian life. Those who are turned in on themselves and go to sleep surrounded by their own possessions, are asked to lift their eyes and to be attentive for the return of the Lord. The beatitude of the believer lies in this: to await the Lord. But the Lord every day stands at the door of our heart and knocks, as is written in the Apocalypse (3:20). Blessed will he be who opens for him because he will have an incredible recompense: the owner himself will become the servant of his servants; he will fasten his belt around himself, and invite his servants to be seated as he passes among them to serve them himself. It is precisely this that Jesus did at the Last Supper. That evening he took a pail of water and a towel and bent down to wash the feet of his disciples, one after the other. Each one of us can relive this example in our prayer, in our service of the poorest, in sharing, in the holy liturgy where the Lord prepares a banquet to nourish us with his word and with his very own life.

Good Night

Before going to sleep think of the gifts received during the day just passed: this will help you not to forget Jesus and to dream of him.

73. Jesus announces that to follow him requires leaving behind one's own ego (Lk 12:49-53)

Jesus, while encouraging his disciples to be vigilant tells them that the moment of decision, of choice, is now. So that the disciples might understand him well he uses the image of fire which he has come to bring upon the earth. The Apocalypse takes up this image when it speaks of the angel who at the end of time will cast fire on the earth (Rv 8:5). Jesus wants his disciples to abandon every inclination they may have to be lazy, slow, cold-hearted and closed in on themselves to embrace his own preoccupation, his own anguish: he is restless until the fires of love have burst into flame in the hearts of men. The disciple therefore is not called to an avaricious and tranquil life, tied solely to personal or communal wellbeing. The disciple must immerse himself in the Gospel and be, as it were, baptized in it. Adhesion to the Gospel requires also a separation from one's former life, based on old ties, even though they may be as strong as that of blood. The Gospel emerges here as a fire that changes the world.

In Another's Shoes

Often we don't take account of how much others do for us in our own families. Today exchange roles: let mother, father and children exchange jobs and each one try to identify him or herself with the other!

74. The disciples must know how to read the "signs of the times" that God offers (Lk 12:54-59)

To those who ask for a sign in order to believe his words, Jesus points to himself as the unique sign that manifests the love of God. But because we are all generally intent solely on ourselves and our own concerns, we do not succeed in seeing the "signs of the Lord," even if they are right before our eyes. This doesn't happen with the heat and the cold: in these cases we lift our eyes to see the clouds and we leave our homes to feel the wind. Analogously we have to be able to understand the time of our salvation. Jesus exhorts us to lift up our eyes, to leave behind the habits that have consolidated and hardened us, in order to distance ourselves from our own egocentrism that renders us blind, in order to be attentive to the signs which the Lord shows us. The first great sign is the Gospel; to listen to it and to put it into practice is the first task of the believer. Then there are the other signs, like the poor and all those who expect to be liberated from the slaveries of the world. To be inattentive to their condition is to say that we do not understand the heart of God and the sense of history.

With Open Eyes

In a moment of relaxation, try to recall all the times your eyes have met another's during the day. Perhaps you weren't paying attention! Tomorrow try to recognize the glance of Jesus in others.

75. Jesus states that it is not God who sends evil on the world (Lk 13:1-5)

Jesus had barely finished speaking to the crowd when some who were there told him about a massacre ordered by Pilate against some Jews who had perhaps attempted an insurrection. This episode offered him the occasion to clarify that certain evils are not the consequence of a fault: those Jews were not guiltier than others who were spared. To clarify Jesus adds another episode about the falling of a tower. God does not send evil, nor does he favor disasters and massacres. On the contrary, God has been in battle against evil from the very beginning, from the time that man appeared in history. And Jesus asks all present to make themselves active in this hard fought battle against evil and the prince of evil. From this followed an appeal to conversion, that is, to a clinging to the Gospel with all one's heart and strength in order to be disciples of Jesus who came into the world to defeat evil and to bring about liberation and salvation.

TV

This evening, the TV has gifted us with a carload of bad news. Offer a simple prayer for the oppressed persons and sad situations present in the world.

76. Jesus exhorts his hearers to pray to the Father who is in heaven (Lk 13:6-9)

This parable illustrates the value of intercession. Occasionally we find ourselves in situations difficult to change: notwithstanding our forces, they remain more or less the same. They resemble that fig tree which does not bear fruit: the owner, for three years, tries to collect its fruit but, not finding any, impatiently goes to the vine grower and tells him to cut it down so that it does not exhaust the soil. This impatience on the part of these "little owners" can take hold of us to the point of depriving us of love and understanding. The vine grower, however, asks the owner to leave it for another year so that he can cultivate and fertilize it; he is certain that the tree will bear fruit. The Lord asks us to have a patience that is wise, to stand by that fig, to surround it with care so that it can bear fruit. We need to learn from God the patience that knows how to hope, that does not extinguish the flickering flame but accompanies those who are weak in order to strengthen them so that they too can contribute to the growth of love.

Patience

Relive your life thinking of the crossroads that were present along your journey and of the patience that, at those times, God and others have had to show towards you.

77. Jesus cures a crippled woman
   ## (Lk 13:10-17)

The Gospel presents us with a woman with a deforming arthritis that has made her curved. For years she has been reduced to this condition; she can't even look others in the face, so great is her curvature. And, as a result, no one looks her in the face. Alone with her problem, she seems resigned to her destiny. How often it happens that the indifference of others convinces us to be resigned to our condition! That woman does not even ask Jesus for a healing as others had done. It is Jesus who is moved by her situation, and he heals her. We can perhaps imagine Jesus as he leans over her to look her in the eye and lift her up. Those who are unmoved are unable to understand even this miracle and they accuse Jesus. But the people understand and praise God for what they have seen.

Dedicate Yourself to Others

Try to better understand what motivates others. Go into your parish or to an association of volunteers and try to find out what are the motives that prompt others to the service of their neighbor.

78. The kingdom of God is small like a seed but it is as efficacious as yeast (Lk 13:18-21)

Confronted by the increasing opposition towards Jesus, doubts about him arise in some people. Is the Gospel too weak for a world that seems to be so very strong? Is it not too simple for a world which seems ever more complex? Confronted by these doubts Jesus tells two parables: that of the grain of wheat and that of the yeast in a loaf of bread. The kingdom of God (that is, the world which God wants to create as a sign of peace, love, justice and mercy) begins precisely like a tiny seed, like a bit of yeast. Certainly it is important that the seed penetrate the soil and that the yeast be mixed into the dough. But both keep their strength and their energy, and if not attenuated by our laziness and our egoism, produce significant fruits: the seed a tall tree, the yeast a new loaf of bread. Many are able to be restored by the shade of our love and to have their hunger taken away by the bread of our mercy.

In the Kitchen

Pick up a good recipe for a pizza baked at home, prepare the dough and wait for it to rise; think of those persons who have been "yeast" in your life. When the dough is ready, all can enjoy a nice pizza together.

79. To choose the kingdom of God requires entering through love's door (Lk 13:22-30)

Luke resumes his theme of a journey towards Jerusalem. He wants to emphasize that the walk of Jesus among men has as its destiny Jerusalem, city of peace and place of salvation. In this context he puts into relief the question surrounding the number of those to be saved, noting that one does not enter into the kingdom by belonging to an ethnic group but by faith. Jesus answers that the door is narrow. Not that the door to God's mercy is narrow; it is we who have enlarged the door to egocentrism to such an extent that there is no room for the Gospel and for love. It is easy to let ourselves be taken up by our own habits, even religious, and to lay claim to them as described in the Gospel pages. And with arrogance, even clothed in humility, pretend a right to attention and esteem. Jesus exhorts us to go through the door of the Gospel: it is narrow for the egoist, but once entered it becomes full of mercy and opens its heart to all people and to all who are looking for salvation.

Reconciliation

Try to experience the mercy of God and, after an attentive examination of conscience, find the time to approach the sacrament of reconciliation.

80. Jesus reprimands the city of Jerusalem because it did not listen to the prophets (Lk 13:31-35)

Jesus has come to the attention of Herod, the ruler of Galilee. Some Pharisees tell Jesus that Herod is looking for him to kill him. This is not the same Herod of the time of Jesus's infancy, but he belongs to the same family. Opposition to the Gospel continues. The evil power of men always fears the power of the Gospel whether it has the weakness of a baby or when it has the weakness of a Word. Jesus could flee to avoid the danger but he does not turn back: he cannot betray the Gospel which is at any rate a Word that is stronger than the power of Herod. The "good news" must be taken inside Jerusalem. Jesus knows well that all of this will cost him his life, but he does not flee and declares: "It is impossible that a prophet should die outside of Jerusalem." He immediately follows this with his sad lamentation over the holy city that does not know how to welcome the word of the prophets, a fact which will lead it to destruction. Only by welcoming the prophecies of God can the life of men, cities and countries find salvation.

Top Secret

Jesus has been courageous. Have we ever risked ourselves for something that seemed right? Write in your "secret diary" the actions of which you are proud or the moment in which you could been done something but did not.

81. Jesus, moved, heals a man with dropsy (Lk 14:1-6)

Jesus was invited, one Sabbath, to a banquet in the house of a Pharisee. From the beginning, the evangelist notes, those present were observing him with hostility. Quite different was the attitude of the crowd which, instead, ran after him to listen to him and to be healed. Among them was a man with dropsy who entered the house and immediately went in front of him. As soon as he saw him Jesus asks the Pharisee if it were lawful or not to heal on the Sabbath. The question was obviously rhetorical and anyway he did not receive an answer. Jesus, without wasting time, healed the sick man. The poor can't wait for disputes and debates. His love and compassion for the weak are without limit and know no bounds. This is the third miracle that Jesus performs on the Sabbath following those that benefitted the man with the withered hand and the woman with a curved back. For Jesus the Sabbath was truly a feast day, a day in which the goodness and love of God for all, especially the weakest, was fully manifested. Every Sunday ought to be like that for us.

Time

Those who have time don't wait! How long has it been since you visited a person with whom you have ties? Today go and pay that person a visit: you can be sure that it will bring them great joy.

82. Jesus condemns the race to take the first place (Lk 14:7-11)

Again Jesus finds himself in the home of a Pharisee who had invited him to dinner. He observes how those invited were choosing the first places. It is a very common happening in life and not only at table: people are forever looking for the first place in the attention and consideration of others. Everyone, beginning with ourselves, has had this experience. But note well the words of Jesus who exhorts us to abstain from seeking the first place; it is not simply an exhortation to have good manners, it is a rule of life. And Jesus clarifies that it is the Lord who gives to each one dignity and honor; it is not we ourselves who give it to them (probably bragging about our doing so in the process). As he did with the beatitudes, Jesus turns upside down the judgment and behaviors of this world. The one who recognizes that he is a humble sinner is exalted by God; the one who instead expects recognition and the first places risks being excluded from the banquet.

In my Place

Today give place to those who come after you in line at the cash register or on the bus or on the train returning home; pay a little attention to someone who has arrived late and doesn't find a place.

83. Jesus tells us to invite the poor when we give a banquet (Lk 14:12-14)

Jesus addresses the Pharisee who had welcomed him into his home and he exhorts him to invite also those who cannot repay him. Once again he overturns the custom: to the meticulous care with which the invited are selected, Jesus contrasts the magnanimity of inviting those who cannot repay and he lists the poor, the blind, the crippled, and the lame. All those, *per se* excluded, Jesus makes participants in the feast. He proposes a totally new concept of the relationship between people, which he is the first to keep: the relationship is based not on reciprocity but on total gratuity, on unilateral love, as the love of God who embraces everyone and especially the poor. And happiness, contrary to what is usually thought, is to be found precisely in opening up the banquet of life to all those excluded without hoping for any recompense. The true recompense will be, in fact, the power to work for this.

A Cup of Coffee

How many times have you seen strangers along the street asking for alms? Try to address a word to them asking them what their name is and where they come from, offering them a cup of coffee or just exchanging some words with them. Perhaps that is what they have most need of after all: to be recognized.

84. The new world of God is a great feast which, refused by some, is open to all (Lk 14:15-24)

Jesus compares the kingdom of God to a great banquet to which numerous guests are invited. But these, when everything is ready, decline the invitation. Each one has his own very understandable excuse: the first has acquired a field and has to go and see it; the second has bought five yoke of oxen and wants to evaluate them; and the third has just celebrated his wedding and it is obvious that he can't come. None of those invited can take part in the feast on account of the improbable responsibilities they have just undertaken. How can you blame them? In truth, wanting to read this passage in greater depth, behind these denials there is a clear decision on the part of those invited: they choose their own thing (the field, the oxen, marriage) and consider that feast entirely secondary. It is true that the excuses offered are serious, but much more serious is the choice for the kingdom of God. The invitation is instead welcomed by the poor and the weak, by the needy and the desperate. These, as soon as they hear the invitation, hasten to answer it and the hall is filled with the invited. For his part Jesus had said: "Blessed are you poor, because the kingdom of heaven is yours" (Lk 6:20).

Take a Pause

How many obligations come up during the day: school, work, sports, various errands, etc.... Try to find an hour in the afternoon to spend in silence, maybe even writing in a diary the reflections that come to you.

85. To follow Jesus it is necessary to renounce one's own ego (Lk 14:25-35)

After a long stay in the house of the Pharisee, Jesus resumes his journey toward Jerusalem followed by a large crowd. Their enthusiasm is palpable. Still he feels the need to clarify with his disciples what it means to be his disciple. He had already spoken of this at the beginning of his trip when he said: "If someone wants to come after me he must deny his very self" (Lk 9:23). Returning to this theme indicates the importance that Jesus attributes to the choice to follow him. He asks that there be an exclusive bond with him, stronger than that which one has with his or her own family. It is in this context that the phrase "to hate" must be understood. The choice to follow him, in other words, has to come before every other affection and concern. It is obvious that all of this requires certain "cuts" that begin precisely in the heart of each one. The exclusive love for Jesus is the foundation for the life of the disciple. If there is not this love it is like building a tower without a foundation and going into battle without an army. Love for Jesus is the substance of the Gospel and it is also that which the disciples must witness to before the world. This love is the salt of life.

Habits

Even for us to follow Jesus requires that we "break" with our old habits. Name one and try to get rid of it.

86. Jesus goes in search of the sheep that has gone astray and the money that is lost (Lk 15:1-10)

Large crowds follow Jesus made up for the most part of the sick, sinners, and abandoned people. And it is obvious that all of this did not pass unobserved. Even more, this privileged relationship with sinners is one of the motives for the accusation: this young prophet mixes too much with them. But Jesus shows that such a relationship is not casual; it forms part of his own mission. More, it reflects the very image of God himself. And he responds to the accusation speaking not of himself but of God, in whom he acts. Chapter 15 is entirely dedicated to the mercy of God. In the first parable God appears as a shepherd who has lost one of his sheep. He leaves the flock in the desert and sets out at once in search of the lost sheep. Both the shepherd and the woman, after having found their lost goods, call in the neighbors and throw a feast. God does not want the death but the life of sinners; for this reason he leaves his home and becomes a beggar for love in Jesus.

For the Parents

The next time your children disobey you, do not yell at them: count to ten, maybe even to twenty, sit down with them and try to talk it out.

87. God is like a father who goes out to meet his lost son who is returning home (Lk 15:11-32)

This parable is known as the parable "of the prodigal son" or "of the merciful father." It is completely centered not on the decisions of the son, but on the unusual behavior of the father who, notwithstanding everything, waits for his younger son to come back home. We all know well, from personal experience, both the attitude of the younger son who prefers to leave home and the love of the father in order to follow his own hopes and desires (repeating the sin of Adam), as well as the harshness of the older son who seeks to defend his privileges without considering even a little the condition of his brother. Both sons are far from the sentiments of the father, who shows mercy without limit toward them. He waits for the younger son to return and as soon as he sees him he runs out to meet him; a gesture for an elderly oriental man that would have been considered not only unusual but also undignified. As well, he also goes out to the older son who doesn't want to come into the house to show his love for and embrace his brother again. "God is like this," Jesus seems to be saying to the Pharisees: he always precedes us in love.

Jealousy

Confronted with a sentiment of jealousy, experienced perhaps in confrontation with a brother or sister, show that you understand well where this feeling comes from. Be strong not to allow yourself to be conquered by it. Ask the Lord to teach you how to accept his love which is totally gratuitous.

88. Jesus exhorts us to do everything possible to bring about a better world (Lk 16:1-8)

Those who listen to the Gospel frequently come across a parable. Jesus, the good and attentive teacher that he is, wants his disciples to understand his words and to embrace them not as an abstract teaching but as words for life. Even on this occasion he takes his cue from a concrete situation: an administrator accused of mismanagement is called in by his master to give an account of his stewardship before he is fired. Jesus, at this point, describes the dishonesty employed by this administrator in order to assure his future and concludes: "The children of this world are more prudent in dealing with their own generation than are the children of light." It is a special exhortation, certainly not to steal, but to act prudently in such a way as to be able to enter the kingdom of God. In other words Jesus exhorts us to the creativity of love and not to resign ourselves before difficulties or to give into our own laziness or resignation. Love knows no limits.

To School

How many of your companions at school are not very likeable? It is difficult to get along with everyone but we must try to do so. From tomorrow on try to speak to at least one of these companions who is more disagreeable, to get to know him or her better: something beautiful might come of it....

89. Jesus warns us against slavery to money and riches (Lk 16:9-18)

Jesus shows his disciples the correct use that one must make of the goods of this earth and of money. He recalls the cleverness of the dishonest administrator who knew how to use money to assure his own future in order to say that even the disciples have to secure their future in the kingdom of heaven. And the way to follow is to make friends with the poor, sharing with them the goods of the earth. They themselves will receive the disciples in the eternal dwelling place. Jesus indicates that love for the weak and the poor is the best way to enter the kingdom. Service to the poor, in fact, far from a pharisaical religiosity which is fundamentally egocentric, liberates from slavery to money (mammon), the font of violence and conflict, and frees one to serve the Lord and his Gospel. The example of Francis of Assisi who went so far as to take off his cloak and give it away, shows us the power and the efficacy of freedom from the goods of the earth.

Sharing

Think of how you might share with the poorest of the poor: give a concrete gift of a partial payment for medicines, or for the sustenance of one who lives far away, or become involved in a beneficial initiative.

90. With the parable of poor Lazarus Jesus shows the way to be merciful towards the poor (Lk 16:19-21)

This text is one of the best known passages from the Gospels. The rich man who dines luxuriously has not been relegated to the past and even Lazarus in not a lost figure. Two persons, two situations. Lazarus with his eyes fixed on the rich man while he waits hoping for some crumbs; and the rich man, instead, who does everything as if Lazarus did not exist, doesn't even see him. Blinded by his riches, he has a blindness which continues to this day in our cities and in our world: a whole population of poor people stands at the doors of the rich, at the doors of life, waiting for some crumbs to fall from the table of those who eat luxuriously. God, instead, chooses Lazarus and calls him by name as if he were a friend so that, even though discarded by men, he can participate in his banquet. For the Lord, and hence for his disciples, the distance between the rich man and Lazarus is an unacceptable scandal and is without any justification. This is to be found in every page of the Scriptures. Even the rich man, if he listened to the word of God and opened his eyes, could recognize the many Lazaruses in this world and be moved by them.

Names

How many poor people do you meet every day along the streets where you walk? Do you know their names? Today ask them who they are and from tomorrow on try to say "Good morning, John," "Good morning, Mary."

91. Jesus tells us to avoid scandal and to forgive (Lk 17:1-4)

Jesus warns his disciples not to give scandal, that is, not to be a stumbling block. He holds that this is such a serious matter as to cause him say that it would be better for those who give scandal to be thrown into the sea with a millstone around their necks. Perhaps the first scandal that the disciples have to avoid is that of contradicting the Gospel with their lives, thus rendering it inefficacious. In these cases what happens is as Jesus had said: "If salt loses its flavor it is no longer good for anything except to be thrown out and trampled underfoot." So be attentive! Listening to the Word, he said to his disciples, keeps sin from becoming attached to you and taking root in your hearts. Jesus then recalls the dimensions of pardon, daily and irremovable in the life of the Christian. Jesus knows well the weakness of his disciples but mercy and forgiveness will super abound in them over sin. To pardon seven times means to pardon always. To forgive must never be lacking in the life of a family of God.

Fragile. Treat with Care

If you should see mom and dad fighting, perhaps even when you are the cause, before going to sleep seek to bring them to peace; with your help it will be easier for them to return to loving one another as before.

92. The apostles ask Jesus to increase their faith (Lk 17:5-10)

"Lord, increase our faith." It is a request that we also make. We know, in fact, that salvation comes from faith, as the entire eleventh chapter of the Letter to the Hebrews describes so well. By faith Abram left his land, by faith Moses liberated the people of Israel from slavery and by faith he brought them to the Promised Land. But faith is not a static reality that one owns like an object. Nor is it adherence to abstract truths. Faith is above all a gift which we receive and which must be kept and cultivated. It is, as St. Paul says, born of hearing. Every day therefore it must be nourished from the Scriptures and must manifest itself in prayer and charity. Jesus, in this Gospel passage says to the disciples that when faith is strong, it is enough to have it as a tiny mustard seed in order to be able to uproot a tree and transplant it in the sea. It is this power that the disciples of Jesus have received from God. Not certainly to take pride in, because we are always useless servants, but to transform the hearts and lives of men.

Corner of Light

Place in a corner of the house an image of Jesus surrounded by seats or cushions. During the day find a time in which to sit together for a moment of prayer and reflection.

93. Jesus heals ten lepers but only one returns to thank him (Lk 17:11-19)

Once again the evangelist takes up the theme of the journey to Jerusalem in order to demonstrate the new climate which springs up among the people when the Lord passes by. When Jesus is about to enter a village he is met by ten lepers. It is the second time that Luke tells about the healing of a leper. This time, different from Luke 5:12-14, the lepers stop at a distance and shout out their need for a cure. It is the cry that rises from many lands, even distant, pleading for help and support. Jesus listens to them and invites them to present themselves to the priests. While they were going there all ten were healed but only one returns to thank the Lord: he is a Samaritan, an outcast, a stranger. The other nine were healed bodily, but their hearts remained sick. Only that Samaritan finds full health. Returning to Jesus and showing his appreciation, he indicates that he does not want to distance himself from the fount of salvation. And he becomes an example even for the disciples, because every day they have to go to the feet of the Lord to thank him for their gifts and blessings.

Thanks

Now is the time to be thankful for a gift received which has not been acknowledged even with a smile: return to the giver and do so now.

94. Jesus says to the disciples that his reign of love is already here (Lk 17:20-37)

The Pharisees ask when the kingdom of God will come. The disciples also ask Jesus a similar question. They are expecting a kingdom like that of the powerful of the earth and they are unaware that the kingdom is already in their midst in the person of Jesus. He initiates the new reign of God, announcing the good news and healing every sickness and infirmity. Evil continues to lose ground and will be definitively conquered by Jesus with his death and resurrection. To choose Jesus and his Gospel is to continue the fight against every manifestation of evil. If men and women, taken up with their own egocentrism, keep indulging themselves excessively and rejecting the proclamation of the Gospel, they are headed for ruin: this is what causes wars and violence which even today continue to destroy life on earth. The disciples are asked to welcome the Lord in their lives and to act with him to extend mercy and love to all.

Urgency

Today help someone by taking his place in undertaking his exhausting job.

95. With the parable of the persistent widow Jesus tells us to pray always without tiring (Lk 18:1-8)

Jesus, from personal experience, knows that the Father always hears him: "Father I thank you that you have heard me; I know that you always hear me," he said before the tomb of Lazarus (Jn 11:41-42). He wants his disciples to be sure, as he is, that prayer is always heard by the Father. And so he tells them the parable of a poor widow who is seeking justice from a judge. This widow, symbol of the impotence of a society like that at the time of Jesus, with her insistence with the judge (dishonest and hardhearted), exhausts him and in the end obtains justice. How much more will your Father in heaven, who is not only just but also has a big heart and is merciful, hear you? The Gospel wants to convince us in every way regarding the strength and power of prayer: when one is persistent one could say that it "obliges" God to intervene. For this reason perseverance in prayer is the first duty of the disciple. Prayer, in fact, has a power such as to change the world.

A Call in Progress

Prayer is like a telephone number to communicate with the Lord: use it to chat with him a little and to thank him.

96. The words of the humble reach God; those of the proud remain on earth (Lk 18:9-14)

Other than perseverance and faith, in prayer humility is necessary. It is easy to place yourself before God like that Pharisee who presumes to be just and trusts only in himself. Faith in oneself replaces faith in God and makes one evil and harsh towards others. The Pharisee goes up to the temple not to ask for help or to seek mercy, but to praise himself and boast before God about his virtues. The tax collector, while being well off and respected, though scorned by many, on the contrary feels himself to be needy and goes up to the temple with empty hands, not to offer but to ask. He is a beggar for forgiveness. For Jesus only the second man is the example of the believer because he does not trust in himself, in his works, his goods or his reputation, but rather only in God. Here again we have an evangelical paradox: "Everyone who exalts himself will be humbled, and the one who humbles himself will be exalted." In fact it is written in the Psalm: "All of us are poor before the Lord."

Quality

Think of some gift that the Lord has given you: think how you have used it, asking pardon if on some occasions you have not valued it as you should.

97. Jesus asks the disciples to let the little children come to him and he blesses them (Lk 18:15-17)

People brought little children to Jesus to have him bless them. They are not the ill in need of healing; all the same contact with Jesus is held, with good reason, to be a real blessing for these little ones. It is significant that, apart from being a nice scene, Jesus lets himself be overwhelmed by the little children, and to his disciples who are upset he says: "Let the children come to me." Yes, let the children know and love Jesus, their true friend. At the time of Jesus little children, like widows, were images of weakness and dependence. Jesus states that the kingdom of heaven is for those who are like them, who recognize their own littleness, for those who do not rely on themselves and entrust everything to God. In this sense those little children become examples for every disciple: it is necessary to approach Jesus and to give oneself to him with the same trust and with the same abandon that those little children had. The disciple will never be an independent adult; he will always remain a child who trusts himself to the Father.

For Parents

Thank the Lord for the surprises that at times are given to you by your children.

98. Jesus also calls the rich to follow him
(Lk 18:18-30)

It isn't a young man, as in the parallel passage in Matthew, but a rich official who approaches Jesus. He calls him Good Master and then he asks what he has to do to obtain eternal life. Jesus comes back at him and says: "Only God is good." It is the first great lesson for us who instinctively consider ourselves, maybe not the "best" but certainly "good." The "bad people," in fact, are always the others. Jesus then continues by listing the commandments. And the official responds saying that he has always kept them, almost as if to say that he expects salvation. He has not understood that salvation is not a question of merits or of buying and selling, but of love. Jesus, then, adds that one thing only is missing: to sell everything, give the proceeds to the poor and to come back and follow him. It is not a matter of sacrifices or of costs. Salvation is born out of exclusive love for the Lord and attention to the poor. That official loved his possessions and did not want to give them up. He went away from Jesus with a sad heart. He didn't understand that true happiness is in following the Lord: in fact God repays by giving us a hundredfold in this world and eternal life in the next.

The Little

Tell about some experience in which you have preferred the little to the more and felt happy about it.

99. Jesus announces his passion to his disciples but they don't want to understand (Lk 18:31-34)

Jesus is getting ever closer to Jerusalem and, for the third time, takes the Twelve apart and confides in them what the conclusion of their journey will be. The evangelist seems to give a particular solemnity to the moment. "Behold we are going up to Jerusalem," Jesus says. There is no doubt that he wants to communicate to them the deepest secret of his life, that of his mission. It is a mission that will unfold according to what is written by the prophets. Jesus is the first, we could say, to obey the Scriptures: everything has to happen according to the will of the Father. Actually it is in Jerusalem that this will of the Father will be fulfilled. Even at the cost of his death. But the Father will not abandon his own Son and, on the third day, he will raise him up. The Twelve are taken up with their own thoughts which are far from those of God; they didn't understand anything. Listening to Jesus is never something mechanical; it always requires abandoning one's own way of thinking, usual positions, and deeply rooted convictions in order to immerse one's self in the thoughts of the other, meditating on their words, taking them to heart, reflecting on them, making them one's nourishment. Only in this way can an individual comprehend and follow the Lord.

Requests

We are all together. Each one should make a request or ask a question. The others listen, don't interrupt, don't judge and try to understand why this particular request was made.

100. Jesus heals the blind man in Jericho who calls out "Help me!" (Lk 18:35-43)

By now Jesus is in the vicinity of Jericho, the last city before Jerusalem. On the road there is a blind man begging for alms. Hearing a lot of noise, he asks what is happening. The people tell him that Jesus of Nazareth is passing by. That man had to get the news from others because he could not see. In effect, all of us have need for someone to announce Jesus to us, who speaks to us of him because we, lost in our own worlds, are like the blind man. Listening to the announcement, the blind man understands that Jesus is not like others who pass by. How many of these had he heard come close, maybe even leave an offering and then continue down the road. From this announcement he understands that Jesus can heal him. For this reason he immediately starts to pray: a simple prayer, but true, because it springs from his need. Jesus listens to that prayer, stops, and has him brought to him. And the dialogue which takes place between Jesus and the blind man concludes with the blind man's healing. That blind man not only sees Jesus with his own eyes, he sees him above all with his heart; in fact he immediately starts to follow him. He is truly an example for all of us.

Messengers

Seek today to be a messenger too for the Lord who is passing by. Each one of us should make it a duty to speak of Jesus at least once during the day.

101. Jesus stops at the house of Zacchaeus and changes his heart (Lk 19:1-10)

Jesus reaches Jericho, the most ancient city in the world and symbol of every city. He didn't enter distracted and in a hurry as is usually the case with us when we are crossing the streets and the plazas of our cities. Jesus is always attentive to people. Zacchaeus, a tax collector and noted sinner, wants to see Jesus but he is very short. He is a little like us, too close to the things of this earth, too preoccupied with our own business to notice Jesus. It's not enough to make a little adjustment, maybe standing on tip toes. It's necessary to go up higher, to leave the confusion of the crowd. Zacchaeus climbs a tree. It was enough to allow him to see Jesus. He wanted very badly to see Jesus but the very opposite happened: Jesus sees him and invites him to come down and to host him in his house. This time a rich man does not go away sad; on the contrary, Zacchaeus gets down out of the tree in a hurry and he welcomes Jesus into his home. Following his meeting with Jesus Zacchaeus is no longer the same. He is happy and has a new, more generous heart. He decides, in fact, to give half of his goods to the poor. He doesn't say: "I give all." He becomes the one invited to welcome the Lord and to find his own measure of charity.

From on High

In a moment of prayer together, ask Jesus to look on some situations that touch your family, your parish, your country.

102. With the parable of the gold coins Jesus exhorts each one of us to spend them out of love (Lk 19:11-28)

Jesus, surrounded by a large crowd, is at the end of his trip and is about to enter Jerusalem. Some thought that the time had come for the manifestation of the kingdom of God, and perhaps held that by now every further effort was useless. But Jesus tells a parable about how to wait for the kingdom. He speaks of a nobleman who leaves his land for a country far away to obtain the dignity of kingship. Before leaving he entrusts to his servants a sum of money so that during his absence they can make it bear fruit. Those servants are obviously not the owners of that sum but administrators who have to act wisely and with diligence. The first two act in this fashion. The third, afraid to risk losing the money, hides the sum without making it bear fruit out of fear of losing his peace of mind and perhaps of being deprived of the care of his own things. He thinks that honesty consists simply in saving the sum that had been entrusted to him. In truth, he lacked familiarity with the owner and hence the co-responsibility he had for the owner's property. He was not even able to enjoy that which he possessed, nor will he hear what was said to the other two: "Good and faithful servant, because you have been faithful in this very small matter, take charge of ten cities."

Fear

Find and acknowledge one of your little fears and once and for all try to overcome it, even asking help from those closest to you.

103. Jesus enters Jerusalem as the good shepherd who changes lives (Lk 19:28-40)

The journey that Jesus had begun in Nazareth is now reaching its conclusion; for many it has been a motive for consolation, healing, comfort, and friendship. And perhaps it is precisely the crowd of the healed, the beneficiaries, the saved, the satiated, the poor, together with the disciples who are celebrating as he enters Jerusalem. Jesus doesn't commandeer a battle horse as the Roman generals or the heads of nations might, nor does he enter on foot as just one of many pilgrims. He sits on a colt, because he is a king, though one of peace, as the prophet Zechariah wrote (Zc 9:9). He is a humble king, strong solely in his meekness. His is the powerful strength of the Gospel that can change the hearts and lives of men. All present acclaim him: "Blessed is he who comes in the name of the Lord; he is the king!" Those who did not acknowledge Jesus as a prophet, now red with fury, go so far as to ask Jesus to silence the disciples, but he responds that if they were to keep quiet, the stones themselves would cry out, so profound is the need for salvation that they had and that we have even today.

Post It

Write a message on the door of your room to remind you that in humility is your strength.

104. Jesus weeps over Jerusalem
(Lk 19:41-44)

Jesus, in seeing Jerusalem, breaks out in tears. More than the simple capital of a State it is the holy city, the goal desired by every Israelite, symbol of the unity of the people. But Jerusalem has betrayed its vocation as the city of peace; anguish and violence run through its streets; the poor are forgotten, the weak are oppressed and above all it is about to reject the prince of peace who has come to visit it: "He came among his own, but his own did not receive him" (Jn 1:11). At the sight of the city, Jesus weeps. He does not weep for himself, as we generally do, but for that city and for the many cities which even today refuse his peace, his justice and his love. Jesus weeps because if they do not welcome the Gospel of love not a stone will remain on another in that city of men. For this, notwithstanding his rejection, Jesus enters Jerusalem as usual, almost as if to breach the walls thrown up against him. He shows that love is stronger than any violence, even the last which is death.

Welcome

Ask yourselves if there is someone whom you have not really "welcomed" and from tomorrow on try to have a different attitude in that individual's regard.

105. Jesus drives the merchants out of the temple (Lk 19:45-48)

Jesus knows what awaits him in Jerusalem, still he does not flee; he enters the city and he makes his way, still with tears in his eyes, toward the temple: it is the heart of the city, the place of the presence of God. But this house of prayer has been transformed into a market place, a place of business, of buying and selling. It is no longer the house of the gratuitous love of God for his people but is rather a place where one could traffic in relationships with God and with men. Jesus, infuriated, drives the sellers out: "My house will be a house of prayer." The only true relationship, the one that has full citizenship in life, is the gratuitous love for God and neighbor. And Jesus, after having driven the merchants out, remains in the temple proclaiming the Gospel every day: the temple begins to be a sanctuary of mercy and of the freely given love of the Lord. Obviously, opposition to the preaching of Jesus on the part of the learned and of those who held a position of some sort, of those who still had the mercantile mentality at heart was not lacking. On the contrary, the poor and the weak, those who had need of everything and lacked the power to claim anything, confronted with the freely-given love of God rushed to Jesus and were "hanging on his words," as Luke notes.

Tone of Voice

Ask yourself if you are careful, when you are discussing among yourselves, not to raise your voice, the one against the other. Let others judge who is right or wrong!

106. Jesus teaches with the authority that comes from God (Lk 20:1-8)

Having driven the merchants out of the temple, Jesus begins to proclaim the Gospel. The temple not only goes back to being a "house of prayer," it becomes the loftiest pulpit of the word of God: "God spoke in times past by means of the prophets; in these days he has spoken to us through his Son" (Heb 1:1-2), writes the author of the Letter to the Hebrews. The authority of that word is undisputed: it not only drove away sellers but it freed the men and women who rushed to listen to it from every kind of slavery and from every ritual, spiritual or social oppression. And still this word, even if full of power, or perhaps because of this, can be rejected. The high priests, the scribes and the elders of the people, in fact, form a kind of conspiracy to block the power of the word. Everything they claimed had to remain as it was, according to the rules that privilege some and oppress the many. The question that they address to Jesus about the origin of his authority risks their being ridiculed, as often happened to those who rejected the Gospel: still they ask it anyway, blind as they are by their self-sufficiency. Only those who recognize their own need know how to welcome the authority of that good Master.

Self-Sufficiency

The need to be authoritative can deceive; goodness knows how to recognize its own limits. Today let others tell you of your defects so that you can become better.

107. The parable of the vine-grower is about opposition to the Gospel (Lk 29:9-19)

Jesus tells this parable in the temple, the religious heart of Israel. We are at the peak of the clash between Jesus and those who oppose him. And Jesus, in an efficacious and tragic synthesis, covers the whole history of the rapport between God and his people, exemplifying it with the image of the vine. The focal point of the parable is made up of the contrast between the expectations of the owner who has not gained anything even though he has cared for and watched over his vineyard patiently in order to obtain its fruits, and the violent reaction of the tenant farmers who, preoccupied only in keeping everything for themselves, mistreating the servants to the point, such is their avarice, of killing the son. Jesus seems to reread the ongoing history of the violent opposition (even outside the Hebraic-Christian traditions) to the servants of God, to the prophets, to the just, to men and women of peace, to the honest people of every time and place, on the part of those who serve only themselves and are subjected to the evil spirit. But the Lord – and here we find the thread of hope which sustains the story – has made his Son the cornerstone of a spiritual edifice that will resist evil. History is not blind and at the mercy of destiny: it is in the hands of God.

If the Seed Does Not Die

Think of some figure in history who has borne fruit "dying," like the seed that bursts into full life only after having been buried in the earth.

108. Jesus says to give to Caesar that which is Caesar's but to God that which is God's (Lk 20:20-16)

Jesus continues teaching in the temple and the opposition to him becomes ever more treacherous. For them, all means are good so long as the Gospel is silenced. What a difference with respect to those who come close to Jesus in order to hear saving words! The opposition presents itself before Jesus in order to catch him in a mistake, even praising him, so as to lead him then before Pilate to ratify his condemnation. These are not pages out of past history: they continue to repeat themselves even today, with the same objective: that the Gospel not be allowed to disturb one's life. The question that they place before Jesus is of a political nature: "Is it licit or not to pay tribute to Caesar?" In the process as reported by Luke they accuse him, falsely, of having interfered with payment of the tax. The response that Jesus gives, in reality, moves on another plane. He says to give to Caesar that which is Caesar's but remember to give to God that which is God's, that is to restore to each man and each woman, made precisely in the image and likeness of God, their true dignity. It is a duty to work so that everyone can recover their first and fundamental identity as children of the one Father, the Lord God.

Politics

Entrust to the Lord, today, someone who works for the common good and is dedicated to political activity. It could be an occasion to send him or her a letter of support or constructive suggestion.

109. Jesus preaches the resurrection which conquers death (Lk 20:27-38)

Jesus is still in the temple. Different from other times, he does not perform any miracle, almost as if to say that his sole strength lies in his word. And, in effect, it is precisely this word that the opposition wants to quiet. It is the Sadducees' turn, the last in the series. Their system of thought denies the resurrection. And it is precisely on this theme that their question turns. The case that they present is mostly artificial, but efficacious: a woman has had seven husbands; of whom will the wife be after her death? They reason according to human logic and rules. But the logic of men is much narrower than that of God. The Gospel shows us a completely new world, comprehensible only to those who open their hearts and minds to God. It is a world where blood ties no longer count because the Spirit transforms them and makes them sublime. It is the world of the risen: there are neither husbands nor wives because all are simply children of the Father. The Father does not abandon his children: the God of Jesus is God of the living, not of the dead. Whoever believes in Jesus is already from this time on "a child of the resurrection." The Father's love is stronger even than death.

Beyond

Visit your dead in the cemetery and recall the moments spent with them. Ask yourself what you think regarding life after death.

110. Jesus presents himself as the Messiah who saves from slavery to sin (Lk 20:39-47)

His answer to the Sadducees received the consent even of the opposition. Now Jesus, by means of the Scriptures, presents himself as the descendant of David, the Messiah. He knows well that this will cost him his life, but he doesn't keep silent. He came for this: to free prisoners, to heal the sick, to proclaim the beginning of the reign of God, a reign of love and peace. For this, addressing himself to those who are listening, he puts the scribes on notice, those of yesterday and those of today. They, while maintaining a religious posture, have as their sole aspiration that of being saluted and of having the first places among men. Loving only themselves they despise everyone else beginning with the poorest and the weakest from whom they cannot pretend to receive anything. It is the story of the rich Dives and poor Lazarus that is ongoing.

Talk Show

   Find a talk show that can stimulate a conversation among yourselves and then discuss the situations proposed.

111. Jesus praises a poor widow who offers two small coins to God (Lk 21:1-4)

Still in the temple, Jesus has just warned those listening to him not to behave like the scribes who make a show of prayer but mistreat widows. While speaking he observes some rich people making a conspicuous offering while a poor widow throws into the treasury two small coins. This gesture and the amount given are totally insignificant with respect to what the rich people gave. And still this gesture, negligible according to the logic of the world, is considered to have eternal value by the Lord. That woman gave everything to God, not keeping anything for herself. Her gesture, in fact, was not born of a theatrical calculation but solely out of a love for her God. She truly loves him with her whole soul, with all her strength, with her whole self, to the point of giving what she has to live on. And her love makes her gesture immortal as every word and good deed done for the weak and the poor is rendered immortal. What to men seems insignificant is rendered eternal by God. For this, we will hear at the end of our lives: "Come, good and faithful servant, because I was hungry and you gave me to eat."

Little Gestures

Pay a visit to someone who is in mourning and spend some time with them. It will be a precious gift that shows attention and closeness.

112. Jesus exhorts his disciples not to waste their days; those that pass will not come back again (Lk 21:5-9)

With this passage Jesus begins his discourse on the end of time (also known as his "eschatological discourse"). But Luke, the evangelist, along with Matthew and Mark, maintains that the "last days" have already begun with Jesus. It is therefore useless to continue putting off the moment of conversion, expecting perhaps another opportune time. The moment to believe the Gospel is this one, so don't lose it. Jesus clearly says that the guarantee of the future, of salvation, is not to be found in the magnificent building of the temple, a human construction, even though it may be religious, but the guarantee of salvation is to be found only in God. For this reason it is necessary to beware of being allured by false prophets as is the manner and customs of this world, and to welcome the only true master of our lives, the Lord Jesus, and our only prophecy, the Gospel. Our whole salvation is to be found herein.

Agenda

Look at last week's agenda (the things to which you gave such importance): were they truly so important? How would Jesus consider them if he were present?

113. Jesus tells his disciples that they will not escape persecution (Lk 21:10-19)

This evangelical text uses the typical apocalyptic language of Scripture to describe the "last days." In reading this page what occurred in the course of the past century comes to mind: we have seen so many tragedies, so much war, genocide, incredible violence, and devastating ruin. And how many persecutions have been directed against believers! The number of martyrs, of every Christian confession, but also of other religions, is extremely high. We can say that the twentieth century was the century of martyrs. It left our present century a legacy of faith to keep and to imitate: these martyrs continue to witness to all of us, often inured by a culture that consumes everything in order to provide individual wellbeing. The Gospel is the most precious treasure that has been handed down to us and which we must transmit to the world. Evil believed that it had won but, with the sacrifice of the martyrs, their blood, their resistance to evil, countless Christians saved the twentieth century from barbarism and now live in the heart of God.

Research

Look for some news about martyrs, even of other religions. Do so not for the pleasure of "knowing about them" but in order to pray together for them and for us.

114. Jesus, with apocalyptic language, describes the tragedies of the world (Lk 21:20-28)

This Gospel passage speaks of the destiny of Jerusalem: to us the present condition of this city, where the Christian community began to take its first steps, comes to mind, along with all its contrasts, as Luke suggests. Jerusalem is the city of these three religions: Judaism, Christianity and Islam. And still it struggles to find peace. We must not forget this. Even for us the words of the Psalm are true: "May my tongue stick to my palate if I forget you Jerusalem" (Ps 137:6). Despite the vision of the heavenly Jerusalem (in the book of Revelation) where all people find themselves gathered around the one God, we find ourselves still tied to this city and, by means of it, to all the cities of the world. The actual disorder in the world, which provokes anguish among people who are uneasy, encourages believers to rise up and lift up their heads because the Son of man is near; more, he has already come and lives in our midst. He can point everyone to the way to peace. It is our responsibility to show the world the Gospel of love.

Peace

Today ask for the gift of peace for those cities of the world that are being tested by violence and war.

115. Jesus exhorts his disciples to be watchful and to pray before difficult situations (Lk 21:29-38)

We are at the vigil of the passion when Jesus will be consigned into the hands of men. And he knows this very well. It is his hour, dramatic as it is. Jesus, we could say, has been preparing himself for his "last days," and he does so proclaiming the Gospel in the temple and retiring at night to the Garden of Olives to pray. "Watch and pray at all times," he tells his disciples in order to resist the recurring power of evil. For Jesus these are not just words; they are rather life. The people sensed this and ran to listen to him beginning very early in the morning. The dawn of a new world seemed about to be born through Jesus. Even today we find ourselves facing difficult situations, at times even very dramatic ones, and we too await the dawn of a new world. The seeds are already there. Jesus tells us, "Look at the fig tree and all the plants." There are many signs even today, some small like seeds, but in them is already present and active a new future, that of the Gospel. Where love, pardon, mercy, dialogue, and peace sprout, there we find the beginnings of the reign of God.

Knots

Today we struggle to be free of those wrongs that we have tied to ourselves; we look for a gesture of forgiveness that can render our heart ever more free.

116. The high priests meet with Judas and plot the death of Jesus (Lk 22:1-6)

They decide on the death of Jesus. The date chosen is that of the Jewish Passover, memorial of the liberation of Israel from slavery under the Egyptians. According to some rabbinical traditions, the Messiah would be alone on the night of the Passover. Now that night was in truth drawing near. But still, once again, as happened at his birth, the Messiah arrives in the midst of the indifference of most and the hostility of many. Jesus will say a little further on: "This is the hour of darkness." The high priests think it to be the most opportune time because the people are distracted by the feast. Satan is at work and the preannounced fixed time has arrived (Lk 4:13). Certainly thirst for money coupled with infidelity conspired in the death of the just one. Jesus had said: "It is not possible to serve two masters, God and Money." The conspiracy against Jesus led by the prince of darkness reaches its conclusion and finds its accomplices.

Experiences

Relate an episode in your life in which all seemed to be "in darkness" and how the moment was overcome and you were able to return to live more serenely.

117. Jesus wants to celebrate the Passover with his disciples (Lk 22:7-13)

Jesus, even though he was aware of the imminence of danger, does not flee Jerusalem. We can imagine what must have passed through his mind in those days; what interior torment he must have undergone in his heart. It is the day of the Unleavened Bread and he wants to celebrate the Passover with his own, with that little group of disciples that he has gathered together and loved. It is a solemn moment for Jesus and it is he himself who gives the disciples the details of the preparations. The parallelism between the narration of this supper and the narration of the entrance of Jesus into Jerusalem underlines the importance given to this moment. Jesus asks that a large room, on an upper floor, be prepared and furnished with couches. One cannot celebrate such an important event in an improvised way. It is a lesson that is given to each one of us, so often scattered and distracted in preparing a place in our hearts for prayer, for listening to the Sacred Scriptures and for celebrating the sacred mysteries. Jesus knows the height and depth of what is about to take place and he has an appropriate setting prepared.

One More Seat

Today prepare with special care the table where the family gets together to eat and put out one extra chair: that will be the seat for a special guest who is Jesus!

118. During the Last Supper Jesus institutes the Eucharist (Lk 22:14-23)

"I have eagerly desired to eat this Passover with you before I suffer." There is an ardent or burning desire on the part of the Lord to be with each one of us. His is not a longing for possession or power; it is the will to create a community based on love and not on competition. For this reason Jesus, even in the anguish of death, stops and sits at table: he wants to experience his work right to the end so that all might come together around him. The bread "given" and the wine "poured out" indicate the total love of Jesus for us, a love that does not hold anything back for himself. This incredible passion causes some questions to rise in us: "And they began to debate among themselves who among them would do such a deed." Not only Judas, but also Peter and the others betray the Lord. To ask yourself about your own love of the Lord is a way of getting over pride, foolishness, the sense of false security, of being a victim, and to begin to open your heart in response to his word. To question ourselves is the beginning of prayer, of listening, of the beginning of new feelings.

Plates

Prepare a special plate, even of a simple loaf of bread, and place it at the center of the table in such a way that each one can serve him or herself in remembrance of this sharing and the communion that Jesus expects from his disciples.

119. Jesus teaches his apostles that the greatest among them is the one who serves the rest (Lk 22:24-30)

The disciples, although always close to Jesus, don't understand a thing with regard to what is taking place. They are not, in fact, paying attention to their master but to themselves, about whom among them is the first, so much so as to initiate an argument between themselves. The argument is in itself a sad fact, but in this moment it becomes a gratuitous act of outrage toward Jesus, because he was not understood in their most profound thoughts. Pride is always outrageous because it blinds and does not let one see or be moved. Jesus, as always, with great patience, continues to teach his disciples the way of love which is different from that which the powerful of the earth follow, who love to govern and often oppress their subjects. For the disciples it must not be this way: "The greatest among you must become the least and the one who governs must be like the one who serves." And Jesus sets for them the example: in the fourth Gospel, with the story of the washing of the feet which took place during the Last Supper, he shows how one exercises primacy among the disciples. And he demonstrates the primacy of love even unto death.

For the Children

You children today should perform an act of service and of assistance to your parents. They do so much for you!

120. Jesus warns Peter that he will deny him three times (Lk 22:31-39)

The Lord addressed Peter with these soothing words: "Don't worry; Satan has asked for all of you but I have prayed for you that, in spite of your weakness, your faith may not fail." But notice the arrogance of Peter: "Lord, I am prepared to go to prison and to die with you." Notice his pride, his aggressive attitude, his sense of security and, in the end, fury. The Lord reminds the disciples, many of whom loved him: "When I sent you forth without a money bag, or a sack or sandals did you lack anything?" They responded: "No." Then he adds: "But now I tell you, those who have a money bag should take it with you, and the same with a sack; the one who does not have a sword should sell his cloak and buy one." These words do not mean that one should buy a money bag and sword, but that a very hard time is soon to be upon them. Not knowing what they were saying, they step forward and say: "Here are two swords." And Jesus, exhausted by his friends' very human way of thinking, says: "Enough!" Once more it is clear how arrogance, aggressiveness, pride and duress render the Gospel mute. The Lord, however, continues to speak to them politely. His ardent passion is not exhausted before the pettiness of their humanity.

For the Parents

Perhaps one of your children needs to be restrained or reprimanded; try to find the words to do this with the greatest tenderness possible.

121. Jesus, in the garden of olives, abandons himself to the will of the Father (Lk 22:39-46)

What causes the grief of the disciples? It comes from their hardness, their pride and aggressiveness. These things have built a kind of wall in their hearts and in their eyes that nothing can penetrate, not even the anguish of the one who is suffering a stone's throw away, praying on his knees. "Why are you sleeping?" The question reaches down to us. "Get up and pray!" This invitation is addressed to us too. But the Lord still remains alone; the angel from heaven who appears to comfort him accuses us of our absence: there is no one to give him comfort, an angel has to come. But Jesus is not thinking of himself even in his anguish. He goes back to his disciples. He knows that his only hope is in the Father who will not abandon him. And so he prays: "If you are willing, Father, take this cup away from me; still, not my will but yours be done." It is the same trust that is apparent in his last words: "Father into your hands I commend my spirit." As the Father did not abandon the people of Israel while they were fleeing from Egypt, so he does not abandon his Son. In the throes of death, in the most complete darkness, the Son knows, even if the reality seems to say the contrary, namely, that his life will not end on the cross.

Media

Pay attention to a story, an event which seems to be somehow caught up in the general indifference and put yourself there instead, at the center of the interests of others.

122. Jesus is arrested in the Garden of Olives (Lk 22:47-53)

Unarmed by choice and refusing the weapons which had been offered to him ("Must we strike with the sword?"), Jesus turns himself over to those who had come to take him with swords and clubs as if he were a criminal. He asks however the reason for such violence against him. It is the violence of the world against the Lord. We cannot deny it, it is in us; it is all around us. And it seems to win. There are moments in the history of humankind, but above all in the history of this people, in which violence seems to have the upper hand. There are moments in the history of Jesus in which violence seems to conquer. "This is your hour and the reign of darkness," Jesus says. And still in the eyes and heart of this man there is profound strength: the strength of him who knows that there will be another, luminous, hour which the Father has prepared. His eyes see with faith a different hour, his heart believes in a different hour, an hour which men cannot guarantee, an hour which the sword cannot give, an hour which only God can give. In that moment the instruments of war will be stilled, the clubs will be thrown away and the light of God will burst forth. But for the moment, at this hour, Jesus is a little man, abandoned into the hands of armed men.

Wounds

Bring to mind a violent act that you have seen or lived through and then think of an act of love received or offered.

123. Peter, in the courtyard of the palace of the Sanhedrin, denies Jesus but then weeps bitterly (Lk 22:54-62)

Confronted by a maid servant and her accusation, Peter betrays his master. Did he lack courage? The problem for the disciple was not that he lacked courage, but that he lacked faith. And faith is something more than courage. The life of the disciple, in fact, is not foolhardy and courageous, but new and different. To have faith means to trust in God and not in self and in one's own strength. Peter finds faith again when the Lord, turning, looks at him. In that moment he recalls the words which Jesus had spoken: "Before the cock crows, you will have denied me three times." And, going out, he weeps bitterly. His faith was born out of his recollection of the words of the Lord. This is more than courage; it is the conviction that we are in the hands of the Lord and that he is leading us to salvation. And if we succumb in a bitter hour, Jesus will lift us up and lead us to the hour of mercy. Peter did not have faith because he had not listened to that which the Lord had said, but when he remembered what he had said, he wept. Those tears were not a sign of courage; they were an expression of faith, a plea for forgiveness. Peter is forgiven because he no longer trusted himself but the Lord.

Remembering

Recall a moment in which your having been forgiven did you good and gave you permission to start over again with greater impetus and trust.

124. Jesus is ridiculed and beaten in the palace of the Sanhedrin (Lk 22:63-65)

Jesus is tortured, ridiculed and beaten. He was also blindfolded; he did not even know who struck him. How many men, how many women, even today, are in places of torture, in the arms of death. How many are blindfolded and don't know to whom the hands of the one who tortured them belong. How many suffer violence in their own body, are blindfolded and don't know where they are going, don't know what to do. Even if they were to cry out no one would hear them, no one could help them. "Prophesy who is it who struck you," the guards taunted Jesus. Like so many others, Jesus fell victim to the verbal abuse of his torturers. There is a hidden part of this world of ours which is full of suffering, sorrow, atrocious torture, and cruel abandonment: it is right to weep over this and to ask that this hour of darkness might pass for them too.

At Table

Before sitting down at table think of one person, one community, one people who are experiencing abandonment and suffering and say a prayer to Jesus that he might give them strength and hope.

125. Jesus appears before the high priest and affirms that he is the Son of God (Lk 22:66-71)

The story of the trial of Jesus develops in various stages. The first is before the council of elders, together with the high priests and scribes. It is a "way of the cross" between the houses of power. And the first is a truly shameful spectacle. These men, even though they refer to God, all seek ways to condemn Jesus to death. The evangelist tells us of the only matter about which Jesus cannot refuse to respond. They ask him if he is the Christ, the Son of God. It's impossible to keep silent before their question, as in fact he will before Herod. In it is encapsulated the whole of the Gospel, the good news spread among the people. Jesus responds: "You yourselves have said so: I am he." We say: what ingenuity he had in answering in this way! But that crafty group of religious men was looking precisely for this. If for Jesus these words are the meat of the Gospel, for them they were blasphemous. And the hands of death were happily clamped on Jesus.

Points to Think About

You are invited, reciprocally, not to judge today, but to use prudence in judging, and to banish from your words and thoughts labels that imprison another.

126. Jesus is taken before Pilate and then Herod (Lk 23:1-12)

Jesus was taken to another palace: that of the representative of Rome. Pilate understands at once that they brought him there out of envy, but he doesn't want to get too mixed up in the internal affairs of the Jews. Knowing that Jesus was a Galilean, he sends him to Herod. Herod does not have any of the juridical harshness of a Roman procurator. He is a curious tyrant who wants to see some miracle, just to be entertained. Jesus is silent. And for this reason Herod felt insulted and ridiculed. This innocent man who calls himself the Son of God becomes condemned on the basis of a law which itself foresaw the coming of the Messiah. Three tribunals were unable to stand up for justice. Jesus is alone and unjustly condemned. Contemplating this Gospel scene we cannot forget those who seek justice and do not find it, those who are brought before tribunals, often summarily and, without compassion, are eliminated. Many times, even today, persons who are enemies among themselves unite to take of advantage of someone who has fallen into their power.

Injustice

Is there a moment in which you felt yourself to be unjustly judged or reprimanded? Today find the courage to say so and to explain the reasons.

127. Pilate, while recognizing that Jesus is innocent, sends him to the cross (Lk 21:13-25)

The sentence of Pilate is clear and Herod agrees: he has done nothing that merits death. "What evil has he done? I have found nothing in him that merits death." Jesus is innocent. In spite of this, he is severely castigated. There is not a single reason to condemn him if not that of giving into the hatred of the few. Against him the current of hate does not cease, it increases like the sea in a tempest: "Crucify him! Crucify him!" It is fanaticism, albeit religious, against him. They want to eliminate him; he is the enemy; it's not worth the trouble to defend him; it's not worth the trouble to spend one's life to plead his cause. And so Pilate releases the man who had been imprisoned for rebellion and murder, for whom they had asked, and he handed Jesus over to them to deal with as they wished. This is the end of the story of Jesus, the story of an innocent man against whom the hatred and fanaticism of the world had been flung. They still did not succeed in placing the tombstone of death over him.

Culpable Silence

Have you ever found yourself in a situation of not wanting to defend someone unjustly accused? What caused you not to speak? Would you do it again?

128. Jesus, on the way of the cross, is aided by Simon of Cyrene (Lk 23:26-34)

Jesus, together with two criminals, takes his last steps with a heavy cross on his shoulder. Seeing him about to die, the soldiers enlist a certain Simon of Cyrene to help him. It is a story of suffering such as unfortunately there has been and is even now in our world. His pain is no different from the pain of the tortured and those condemned to death; it is not different from the suffering of the sick today, of the abandoned. There is very little to say about this suffering: we must seek an answer to it within ourselves; it offers us an opportunity to share in the suffering of Jesus with a compassion which the world is unable to muster. Not even sensitive persons like the women of Jerusalem who, while weeping and lamenting, manage to fully share in it. But there are some words here which strike us in a special way; they are those of Jesus: "Father, forgive them because they know not what they do." Even the assassins of the Son of God can be pardoned, and with them all of us. From the cross there comes an invitation to all to work so that death and violence no longer reign.

For the Parents

Tell your children about the weight of some problems and sad situations which you have had to face. Ask them to share a little with you in these your thoughts and sentiments.

129. Jesus promises paradise to the good thief and dies (Lk 23:35-49)

The last words of Jesus are the words of him who trusts the Father: they seem to be the last but in reality they initiate him into a new life pronounced after a "No" and following a "Yes." The "No" is to the teaching of this world: "Save yourself!" which everyone was shouting: the leaders of the people, the soldiers and even one of the two men crucified with him. "No," the Lord replies. How could he save himself, he who had come to save the others? And then there is the "Yes" to the anguish of this world, and to one of the thieves who said to him: "Remember me." His last breath is to respond "Yes" to this evildoer. A great darkness came over the whole land from noon until three, and Jesus says: "Father into your hands I commend my spirit." This scene bothers many of those present: the centurion, the acquaintances who were standing at a distance and the people who returned home beating their breasts. This scene from the Gospel continues to disturb us too.

A Difficult "Yes"

In order to interiorize the "Yes" of Jesus let us also say "Yes" to a difficult obligation we may have to face today.

130. Jesus is buried in a new tomb
(Lk 23:50-56)

A good and just man did not go along with the decision to kill Jesus: and out of his refusal to go along a gesture of piety was born. Another Joseph comes along at the end of the life of Jesus; he takes him down from the cross and wraps him in a linen cloth placing him in a new sepulcher. Some women who had followed Jesus join him. Luke writes that before the tomb, the sorrow, and the death, before the disciples went to sleep, before all the suffering, only faith in the words of Jesus that he had entrusted himself entirely to the Father remain. It was the day of preparation and the Sabbath was about to begin. The women were perhaps not the only ones in the city who got up early but also those expecting a new hour, a new day for that man and for the world. In the presence of such great sorrow, those who did not agree with the decision to kill and oppress him were asked not so much to weep as to believe, to pray, to hope in a new and different hour.

Post-It

Let each one place on the refrigerator a phrase or a prayer to help in believing and hoping for "a different hour" in a difficult situation.

131. Some women, arriving at the tomb, receive the news that Jesus had risen (Lk 24:1-12)

Some women arrived at the tomb early in the morning, but they found it open and empty. Two angels appeared to them and said: "Why do you seek the living among the dead?" But where, if not among the dead, would one look for Jesus? Where would you seek one who had been condemned by everyone? One who had been abandoned by his own? The angels insist: "He is not here, but he has been raised. Remember what he said to you while he was still in Galilee." The women recalled the words of Jesus and believed. Faith, as we have said, comes from listening. And they listened and became the first witnesses to the resurrection. They are living an incredible hour: the one who had been defeated, lives. They ran to tell the apostles who think that the women are daydreaming. Jesus had conquered death; he did so without money, without hatred, without violence. He conquered with love. Each person who accepts this Gospel will live, because the love of Jesus is stronger than death.

The Cross

Buy some flowers and bring them to church and place them before Jesus crucified.

132. Two disciples returning to Emmaus recognize the risen Jesus (Lk 24:13-35)

Two disciples, saddened, return to their village to take up once more the monotony of their everyday life. Motives for being sad are not lacking: the Gospel had been defeated, hatred had conquered love, evil had conquered the good, and indifference had overcome compassion. But a stranger approaches them and begins to explain the Scriptures to them. Little by little as they listen, their hearts begin to burn within them. Toward the end of the trip there arises in their hearts a simple prayer: "Stay with us." The stranger stays; he sits at table with them and breaks the bread. At that moment their eyes are opened and they recognize Jesus. The story of these two disciples is emblematic of every believer. They were not apostles, and we don't even know the name of one of them. In the story we are shown the way to encounter the Risen One: listen to the Scriptures and take part in the Eucharistic meal.

For Couples

Perhaps it has been a good while since you have found time exclusively for yourselves? Set aside a little time, just the two of you, to relive the moments in which you felt the presence of the Lord at your side.

133. At the end of Easter, the risen Jesus appears to his disciples locked in the cenacle (Lk 24:36-43)

Finally, Jesus appears to the apostles. We are at the close of the day of the resurrection. Jesus early in the morning was with the women, then he spent the rest of the day with the two from Emmaus and only in the evening does he present himself to the apostles. They are locked in the cenacle out of fear. It is a fear that we know all too well: how many times have we closed the doors of our heart out of fear of losing something! But Jesus once again enters and places himself in their midst. Not off to one side, but in their midst, in the center. He says: "Peace be with you!" The disciples think that it is a ghost. They had heard the women and then the two from Emmaus, but fear is still strong in them. Incredulity, the evangelist seems to say, is with us always. And Jesus insists that it is he by then showing them his hands and his feet with their wounds, almost as if to say that after listening mercy must follow; it is necessary, that is, to touch with one's own hands the wounds still present in the world; it is necessary to go forth to encounter those who suffer in order to be able to understand what the resurrection is trying to say to us.

Peace

What kind of gesture of peace can you make today towards others so that they might feel in their hearts the words of Jesus: "Peace be with you"?

134. Jesus sends the disciples into the world to communicate to all the Gospel of love (Lk 24:44-49)

Jesus is about to return to the Father and leaves to his own his last instructions. To the apostles he entrusts the work of continuing his mission. They are a small and frightened group. Jesus conquers their fear by opening their minds to an understanding of the Scriptures. It is as he had done with the two from Emmaus; it is what he did with the apostles in the cenacle, and it is what he continues to do even with us. The Gospel is the disciples' only treasure; and they must witness to it to the ends of the earth. But they will not be abandoned to themselves and to their meagre strength. They will be clothed with power from on high. They will receive the Holy Spirit, the fire of love that will overcome their fears and burn away every limit they may encounter. It is love that changes the world.

Fear

Ask yourself if you are afraid to witness to your faith in public. Then take it upon yourself to do so without shame because Jesus needs even you.

135. Jesus is taken up to heaven and gives the disciples the joy of continuing his mission (Lk 24:50-53)

We have come to the end of the Gospel. Jesus goes out with his disciple to Bethany and while he blesses them he is taken up to heaven. After the disappearance of Jesus, they return to Jerusalem with great joy. How can they rejoice in the absence of Jesus? The disciples understand that Jesus is risen and that from that moment on he will always be close to them and to the disciples of every age and place. Going up to heaven, in fact, he surrounds the life of every person, as the heavens surround the earth. Each day they are found in the temple praying and praising God. Thus the story of the Church and of every Christian community begins: being together in listening to the Scriptures and in praying. The Gospel of Luke does not end here, but continues with the narration of the Acts of the Apostles and with the acts of all the disciples of every age, even our own.

Little Gestures

Each one should make a little sign of the cross on the forehead of another, blessing that person in the name of the Lord.

ST PAULS

This book was produced by ST PAULS, the publishing house operated by the Society of St. Paul, an international religious congregation of priests and brothers dedicated to serving the Church through the communications media.

For information regarding this and associated ministries of the Pauline Family of Congregations, write to the Vocation Director, Society of St. Paul, 2187 Victory Blvd., Staten Island, New York 10314-6603. Phone us at 718 865-8844.

E-mail: vocation@stpauls.us
www.vocationoffice.org

That the Word of God be everywhere known and loved.